MW01257473

THE EASTERN PRAYER BOOK

Prayers for Various Occasions
Including Divine Liturgy

Compiled by Theophilus Floyd
Adapted from both Greek and Russian Sources

THE EASTERN PRAYER BOOK

Prayers for Various Occasions, Including Divine Liturgy

The prayers of the Eastern Orthodox and Byzantine Rite Church, arranged according to the daily flow of prayer life, including Akathists, General Prayers, and the Divine Liturgy of Saint John Chrysostom.

This edition has been formatted for use by individuals or for general parish use. The easy to read design and the notations are intended to help facilitate attention in your prayer life. Ruberics are included. Most locations where the Reader, Priest or Congregation are to make the sign of the cross have been indicated with a cross.

This prayer book remains under constant revision, and more prayers, akathists, canons and prayers will continue to be added in subsequent editions. To receive all of these updates for free, it is advisable to purchase the Kindle version which will be updated automatically at no extra charge.

If you have any suggestions for additions, please contact the author directly via Facebook or Google+.

facebook.com/Theophilus79
plus.google.com/u/0/+TheophilusFloyd

All contents have been compiled by Theophilus Floyd, M.Sc. from both Greek and Russian sources (see last page) and reformatted for ease of reading.

TABLE OF CONTENTS

MATINS

"O God, Thou art my God; early will I seek Thee!" - Psalm 63

At dawn the believer again rises and seeing the coming of day, the expression of God's abundant love towards mankind and all creation, he or she goes first to God with praises, thanksgivings and petitions, seeking His blessing for the new day. From the old Israel, Christians inherited the discipline of prayer at set times of the day. The Church, the new Israel, through the life-giving Spirit, established Matins fully as the prayer of sunrise.

Glory to God in the highest, and on earth peace, good will towards men.
Glory to God in the highest, and on earth peace, good will towards men.
Glory to God in the highest, and on earth peace, good will towards men.

✠ Heavenly King, Comforter, True Spirit, Who art everywhere and fillest all, Treasury of good things and Giver of life: come and dwell within us, and cleanse us from every impurity, and save our souls, O Good One. *(Bow)*

TRISAGION PRAYERS

✠ Holy God! Holy Mighty! Holy Immortal! Have mercy on us. *(Bow)*
✠ Holy God! Holy Mighty! Holy Immortal! Have mercy on us. *(Bow)*
✠ Holy God! Holy Mighty! Holy Immortal! Have mercy on us. *(Bow)*

✠ Glory to the Father and to the Son and to the Holy Spirit, now and
ever and unto ages of ages. Amen. *(Bow)*

THE LORD'S PRAYER

Our Father Who art in heaven, hallowed be Thy name. Thy kingdom come. Thy will be done, on earth as it is in heaven. Give us this day our daily bread. And forgive us our trespasses, as we forgive those who trespass against us. And lead us not into temptation, but deliver us from the evil one.

For Thine is the kingdom and the power and the glory, of the ✠ Father and of the Son and of the Holy Spirit, now and ever and unto the ages of ages. Amen.

PSALM 3

O Lord, why are they multiplied that afflict me? Many rise up against me.

Many say unto my soul: There is no salvation for him in his God.

But Thou, O Lord, art my helper, my glory, and the lifter up of my head.

I cried unto the Lord with my voice, and He heard me out of His holy mountain.

I laid me down and slept; I awoke, for the Lord will help me.

I will not be afraid of ten thousands of people that set themselves against me round about.

Arise, O Lord, save me, O my God, for Thou hast smitten all who without cause are mine enemies; the teeth of sinners hast Thou broken.

Salvation is of the Lord, and Thy blessing is upon Thy people.

I laid me down and slept; I awoke, for the Lord will help me.

PSALM 37

O Lord, rebuke me not in Thine anger, nor chasten me in Thy wrath.

For Thine arrows are fastened in me, and Thou hast laid Thy hand heavily upon me.

There is no healing in my flesh in the face of Thy wrath; and there is no peace in my bones in the face of my sins.

For mine iniquities are risen higher than my head; as a heavy burden have they pressed heavily upon me.

My bruises are become noisome and corrupt in the face of my folly.

I have been wretched and utterly bowed down until the end; all the day long I went with downcast face.

For my loins are filled with mockings, and there is no healing in my flesh.

I am afflicted and humbled exceedingly, I have roared from the groaning of my heart.

O Lord, before Thee is all my desire, and my groaning is not hid from Thee.

My heart is troubled, my strength hath failed me; and the light of mine eyes, even this is not with me.

My friends and my neighbors drew nigh over against me and stood, and my nearest of kin stood afar off.

And they that sought after my soul used violence; and they that sought evils for me spake vain things, and craftiness all the day long did they meditate.

But as for me, like a deaf man I heard them not, and was as a speechless man that openeth not his mouth.

And I became as a man that heareth not, and that hath in his mouth no reproofs.

For in Thee have I hoped, O Lord, Thou wilt hearken unto me, O Lord my God.

For I said: Let never mine enemies rejoice over me; yea, when my feet were shaken, those men spake boastful words against me.

For I am ready for scourges, and my sorrow is continually before me.

For I will declare mine iniquity, and I will take heed concerning my sin. But mine enemies live and are made stronger than I, and they that hated me unjustly are multiplied.

They that render me evil for good slandered me, because I pursued goodness.

Forsake me not, O Lord my God, depart not from me. Be attentive unto my help, O Lord of my salvation. *(Two Times)*

PSALM 62

O God, my God, unto Thee I rise early at dawn.

My soul hath thirsted for Thee; How often hath my flesh longed after Thee in a land barren and untrodden and unwatered.

So in the sanctuary have I appeared before Thee to see Thy power and Thy glory, For Thy mercy is better than lives; my lips shall praise Thee.

So shall I bless Thee in my life, and in Thy name will I lift up my hands.

As with marrow and fatness let my soul be filled, and with lips of rejoicing shall my mouth praise Thee.

If I remembered Thee on my bed, at the dawn I meditated on Thee. For Thou art become my helper; in the shelter of Thy wings will I rejoice.

My soul hath cleaved after thee, thy right hand hath been quick to help me.

But as for these, in vain have they sought after my soul; they shall go into the nethermost parts of the earth, they shall be

surrendered unto the edge of the sword; portions for foxes shall they be.

But the king shall be glad in God, everyone shall be praised that sweareth by Him; for the mouth of them is stopped that speak unjust things.

At the dawn I meditated on Thee. For Thou art become my helper; in the shelter of Thy wings will I rejoice.

My soul hath cleaved after Thee, Thy right hand hath been quick to help me.

Glory to the Father, and to the Son, and to the Holy Spirit, both now and ever, and unto the ages of ages. Amen.

Alleluia, alleluia, alleluia. Glory to Thee, O God. *(Three Times)*

Lord, have mercy. *(Three Times)*

✚ Glory to the Father, and to the Son, and to the Holy Spirit, both now and ever, and unto the ages of ages. Amen.

PSALM 87

O Lord God of my salvation, by day have I cried and by night before Thee.

Let my prayer come before Thee, bow down Thine ear unto my supplication.

For filled with evils is my soul, and my life unto hades hath drawn nigh.

I am counted with them that go down into the pit; I am become as a man without help, free among the dead, like the bodies of the slain that sleep in the grave, whom Thou doest remember no more, and they are cut off from Thy hand.

They laid me in the lowest pit, in darkness and in the shadow of death.
Against me is Thine anger made strong, and all Thy billows hast Thou brought upon me.

Thou hast removed my friends afar from me; they have made me an abomination unto themselves.

I have been delivered up, and have not come forth; mine eyes are grown weak from poverty.

I have cried unto Thee, O Lord, the whole day long; I have stretched out my hands unto Thee.

Nay, for the dead wilt Thou work wonders? Or shall physicians raise them up that they may give thanks unto Thee?

Nay, shall any in the grave tell of Thy mercy, and of Thy truth in that destruction?

Nay, shall Thy wonders be known in that darkness, and Thy righteousness in that land that is forgotten?

But as for me, unto Thee, O Lord, have I cried; and in the morning shall my prayer come before Thee.

Wherefore, O Lord, dost Thou cast off my soul and turnest Thy face away from me?

A poor man am I, and in troubles from my youth; yea, having been exalted, I was humbled and brought to distress.

Thy furies have passed upon me, and Thy terrors have sorely troubled me.

They came round about me like water, all the day long they compassed me about together.

Thou hast removed afar from me friend and neighbour, and mine acquaintances because of my misery.

O Lord God of my salvation, by day have I cried and by night before Thee.
Let my prayer come before Thee, bow down Thine ear unto my supplication.

PSALM 102

Bless the Lord, O my soul, and all that is within me bless His holy name.

Bless the Lord, O my soul, and forget not all that He hath done for thee,

Who is gracious unto all thine iniquities, Who healeth all thine infirmities,

Who redeemeth thy life from corruption, Who crowneth thee with mercy and compassion,

Who fulfilleth thy desire with good things; thy youth shall be renewed as the eagle's.

The Lord performeth deeds of mercy, and executeth judgment for all them that are wronged.

He hath made His ways known unto Moses, unto the sons of Israel the things that He hath willed.

Compassionate and merciful is the Lord, long-suffering and plenteous in mercy; not unto the end will He be angered, neither unto eternity will He be wroth.

Not according to our iniquities hath He dealt with us, neither according to our sins hath He rewarded us.

For according to the height of heaven from the earth, the Lord hath made His mercy to prevail over them that fear Him.

As far as the east is from the west, so far hath He removed our iniquities from us.

Like as a father hath compassion upon his sons, so hath the Lord had compassion upon them that fear Him; for He knoweth whereof we are made, He hath remembered that we are dust.

As for man, his days are as the grass; as a flower of the field, so shall He blossom forth.

For when the wind is passed over it, then it shall be gone, and no longer will it know the place thereof.

But the mercy of the Lord is from eternity, even unto eternity, upon them that fear Him.

And His righteousness is upon sons of sons, upon them that keep his testament and remember His commandments to do them.

The Lord in heaven hath prepared His throne, and His kingdom ruleth over all.

Bless the Lord, all ye His angels, mighty in strength, that perform His word, to hear the voice of His words.

Bless the Lord, all ye His hosts, his ministers that do His will.

Bless the Lord, all ye His works, in every place of His dominion.

Bless the Lord, O my soul.

In every place of His dominion, bless the Lord, O my soul.

O Lord, hear my prayer, give ear unto my supplication in Thy truth; hearken unto me in Thy righteousness.

And enter not into judgment with Thy servant, for in Thy sight shall no man living be justified.

For the enemy hath persecuted my soul; He hath humbled my life down to the earth.

He hath sat me in darkness as those that have been long dead, and my spirit within me is become despondent; within me my heart is troubled.

I remembered days of old, I meditated on all Thy works, I pondered on the creations of Thy hands.

I stretched forth my hands unto Thee; my soul thirsteth after Thee like a waterless land.

Quickly hear me, O Lord, my spirit hath fainted away. Turn not Thy face away from me, lest I be like unto them that go down into the pit.

Cause me to hear Thy mercy in the morning; for in Thee have I put my hope.

Cause me to know, O Lord, the way wherein I should walk; for unto Thee have I lifted up my soul.

Rescue me from thine enemies, O Lord; unto Thee have I fled for refuge.

Teach me to do Thy will, for Thou art my God. Thy good Spirit shall lead me in the land of uprightness; for Thy name's sake, O Lord, shalt Thou quicken me.

In Thy righteousness shalt Thou bring my soul out of affliction, and in Thy mercy shalt Thou utterly destroy mine enemies.

And Thou shalt cut off all them that afflict my soul, for I am Thy servant.

Hearken unto me, O Lord, in Thy righteousness, and enter not into judgment with Thy servant. *(Three Times)*

Thy good Spirit shall lead me in the land of uprightness.

✚ Glory to the Father, and to the Son, and to the Holy Spirit, both now and ever, and unto the ages of ages. Amen.

Alleluia, alleluia, alleluia. Glory to Thee, O God. *(Three Times)*

PRAYERS

We praise Thee, we hymn Thee, we bless Thee, and we give thanks unto Thee, O God of our fathers, for Thou hast led us through the darkness of the night, and hast shown unto us again the light of day. But we entreat Thy goodness: Do Thou cleanse us from our sins and accept our supplication, according to Thy great compassion, for we flee unto Thee, the merciful and all powerful God. Shine in our hearts the true Sun of Thy Righteousness, illumine our mind and guard all our senses, that walking uprightly, as in the day, in the way of Thy commandments, we may attain unto life eternal (for with Thee is the fountain of life), and be counted worthy to come unto the enjoyment of Thine unapproachable light.

For Thou art our God, and unto Thee do we send up glory: to the ✚ Father, and to the Son, and to the Holy Spirit, now and ever, and unto the ages of ages. Amen.

THE DOXOLOGY

Glory to God in the highest, and on earth peace, good will towards men!

We praise Thee, we bless Thee, we worship Thee, we glorify Thee, we give thanks to Thee for Thy great glory.

O Lord, Heavenly King, God the Father Almighty; O Lord, the Only-begotten Son, Jesus Christ; and O Holy Spirit. O Lord God, Lamb of God, Son of the Father, that takest away the sin of the world, have mercy on us;

Thou that takest away the sins of the world, receive our prayer; Thou that sittest at the right hand of the Father, have mercy on us.

For Thou only art holy, Thou only art the Lord, Jesus Christ, to the glory of God the Father. Amen.

PRAYERS

Every day will I bless Thee, and I will praise Thy name for ever, yea, for ever and ever. Vouchsafe, O Lord, to keep us this day without sin. Blessed art Thou, O Lord, the God of our Fathers, and praised and glorified is Thy name unto the ages. Amen. Let Thy mercy, O Lord, be upon us, according as we have hoped in Thee.

Blessed art Thou, O Lord, teach me Thy statutes. *(Three Times)*

Blessed art Thou, O Master, make me to understand Thy commandments.

Blessed art Thou, O Holy One, enlighten me with Thy precepts.

Thy mercy, O Lord, endures forever. Do not despise the works of Thy hands.

To Thee belongs worship! To Thee belongs praise! To Thee belongs glory!

To the ✚ Father and to the Son and to the Holy Spirit, now and ever and unto ages of ages. Amen.

Through the prayers of our ✚ holy fathers, may the Lord have mercy on us. Amen.

MORNING PRAYERS

In the morning, having risen from sleep, make the Sign of the Cross, saying the Jesus Prayer, which is:

✚ Lord Jesus Christ, Son of God, have mercy on me, a sinner. *(Bow)*

Having risen from the bed and washed your face, stand before the holy icons, and looking upon them, turn your thoughts to the invisible God.

THE ENTRANCE BOWS

Then, guarding yourself with the Sign of the Cross and making bows, say with compunction the Prayer of the Publican:

God be merciful to me a sinner. *(Bow)* Thou hast created me; Lord, have mercy on me. *(Bow)* I have sinned immeasurably; Lord have mercy and forgive me a sinner. *(Bow)*

It is truly meet to bless thee, O ✚ Theotokos, the ever-blessed and most immaculate, and the Mother of our God. More honorable than the cherubim and truly more glorious than the seraphim; thee who without defilement gavest birth to God the Word, the true Mother of God, thee do we magnify. *(Bow)*

✚ Glory to the Father, and to the Son, and to the Holy Spirit. *(Bow)* Now and ever, and unto the ages of ages. Amen *(Bow)*

Lord, have mercy. Lord, have mercy, Lord, bless. *(Bow)*

DISMISSAL

Lord Jesus Christ, Son of God, through the prayers of Thy most pure Mother, by the power of the precious and life-giving Cross, through the prayers of my holy Guardian Angel, and of all the saints, have mercy on me and save me a sinner, for Thou art good and lovest mankind. *(Bow)*

These Entrance Bows are made whenever one enters the church to stand in prayer. Whenever one has finished praying and is about to leave the church, he makes the Departure Bows (in the same manner). And when one is about to leave his home, he also makes the aforementioned bows.

Through the prayers of our holy fathers, Lord Jesus Christ, Son of God, have mercy on us. Amen. *(Bow)*

✚ Glory to Thee, our God, Glory to Thee for all things. *(Three Times)*

1st PRAYER OF SAINT MACARIUS THE GREAT

O God, cleanse me a sinner, for I have done nothing good before Thee. Deliver me from the Evil one, and may Thy will be in me, that I might open my unworthy lips without condemnation and praise Thy holy name, Father, Son and Holy Spirit, both now and forever and unto ages of ages. Amen.

2nd PRAYER OF SAINT MACARUIS THE GREAT

Having risen from sleep, I offer Thee, O Savior, the midnight song. Falling down, I cry to Thee: let me not fall asleep in the death of sin. Be gracious to me, Thou Who wast willingly crucified. Raise me quickly as I lie in laziness, and save me as I stand in prayer. After the night's sleep, O Christ God, shine a sinless day upon me and save me.

3rd PRAYER OF SAINT MACARIUS THE GREAT

Having risen from sleep, I run to Thee O Master, for Thou lovest mankind, and I rush to accomplish Thy work. Help me, I pray Thee, at all times and in all things. Deliver me from every evil thing of this world, and from works of the devil. Save me, and lead me into Thine eternal Kingdom. Thou art my Maker, the Provider and Giver of everything good. All my hope is in Thee and I glorify Thee, now and forever and unto ages of ages. Amen.

4th PRAYER OF SAINT MACARIUS THE GREAT

O Lord, through Thy abundant goodness and great generosity, Thou hast allowed me, Thy servant, to pass through the hours of this night untempted by any evil of the enemy. Grant also, O Master and Creator of all, that I might accomplish Thy will in Thy true light and with an illumined heart, now and forever and unto ages of ages. Amen.

5th PRAYER OF SAINT MACARIUS THE GREAT

O Lord, the Almighty God, Who acceptest the three times holy hymn from Thy heavenly hosts: accept this song of the night even from me, Thine unworthy servant. Grant that at every year and hour of my life I might glorify Thee, the Father, the Son and the Holy Spirit, now and ever and unto ages of ages. Amen.

6th PRAYER OF SAINT BASIL THE GREAT

Almighty Lord, the God of hosts and of all flesh, Thou livest in the heights, yet lookest down on the humble, proving the hearts and emotions, clearly foreknowing the secrets of men. Thou art the Light without beginning, in Whom there is neither variation nor shadow of change. O Immortal King, accept the prayers which we now offer Thee from defiled lips. Free us from the sins we have committed in deed, word or thought, knowingly and unknowingly. Cleanse us from all defilement of flesh and spirit. Grant us to pass through the entire night of this present life with a watchful heart and a sober mind, awaiting the coming of the bright and manifest day of Thin only begotten Son, our Lord, God and Savior Jesus Christ, when the Judge of all will come with glory to reward each according to his deeds. May we not be found fallen and lazy, but alert and roused to action, prepared to enter into His joy and the divine chamber of His glory, where the voice of those who feast is unceasing and indescribable is the delight of those who behold the inexpressible beauty of Thy countenance. For Thou art the true Light which enlightens and sanctifies all, and all creation hymns Thee unto ages of ages, Amen.

7th PRAYER OF SAINT BASIL THE GREAT

We bless Thee, most high God and Lord of mercies, Whoever doth do great and unfathomable things for us. Glorious and awesome things without number. Thou givest us sleep for the repose of our frailty, relieving the labors of our overburdened flesh. We thank Thee for not destroying us in our lawlessness. Instead, Thou hast shown Thy usual love for mankind, and raised us, as we lay in despair, to glorify Thy Reign. Therefore, we implore Thy boundless goodness: enlighten our thoughts and eyes, and awaken our minds from the heavy sleep of laziness. Open our lips and fill them with Thy praise, that we may unwaveringly hymn and confess Thee, the God glorified in all and by all, Father without beginning, with Thine only begotten Son and Thine all holy and life giving Spirit, now and forever and unto ages of ages. Amen.

TO THE HOLY TRINITY:

Having arisen from sleep, we fall down before Thee, O Blessed One, and sing to Thee, O Mighty One, the angelic hymn: Holy! Holy! Holy! art Thou, O God; through the ✚ Theotokos, have mercy on us.

✚ Glory to the Father, and to the Son, and to the Holy Spirit.

Do Thou, O Lord, who hast raised me from my bed and from sleep, enlighten my mind and heart, and open my lips that I may praise thee, O Holy Trinity: Holy! Holy! Holy! art Thou, O God; through the ✚ Theotokos, have mercy on us.

Now and ever and unto ages of ages. Amen.

The Judge will come suddenly and the acts of every man will be revealed; but with fear we cry in the middle of the night: Holy! Holy! Holy! art Thou, O God; through the ✚ Theotokos, have mercy on us.

TO THE FATHER:

O Lord Almighty, God of hosts and of all flesh, dwelling in the highest, caring for the humble, searching the reins and the heart, and clearly discerning the hidden things of men: O unoriginate and ever-existing Light, with whom there is no variation or shadow due to change. Do Thou, O immortal King, accept our prayers which we offer to Thee at this present time from our soiled lips, trusting in the multitude of Thy bounties; forgive us our transgressions which we have committed knowingly or unknowingly, whether in word or deed or thought; cleanse us from all stain of body and soul. Grant us to pass through all the night of this present life with vigilant heart and sober thought, awaiting the coming of the radiant and manifest Day of Thy only begotten Son, our Lord and God and Savior Jesus Christ, on which the judgment of all men shall come with glory, when to each man shall be given the reward of his deeds. May we not fall and become lazy, but instead have courage that, being roused to action, we may be found ready to enter into the joy and the divine bride-chamber of His glory, where the voice of those who feast is unceasing, and the gladness of those who behold the goodness of Thy countenance is unending. For Thou art the True Light who enlightenest and sanctifiest all things, and all creation sings Thy praise forever, Amen.

TO THE THEOTOKOS:

I sing the praises of your grace, O Lady, entreating you to enrich my mind with grace! Teach me to walk uprightly, in the Way of Christ's commandments. Strengthen my vigilance in song and prayer, which drive away the despair of sleep. Free me by your entreaties, O Bride of God, who art bound by sinful garments. Protect me in the night and in the day, delivering me from the enemies who con- tend against me. Give life to me who have been deadened by passion, you that gave birth to the life giving God. Enlighten my blinded soul, you that gave birth to the never-ending Light. O wonderful Palace of the Master, make me a house of the Divine Spirit. You that gave birth to the Physician, make well the passions of my soul. Lead me, who am bestormed by life, to the ways of repentance. Deliver me from the eternal flames. Do not show me to the joy of demons because of my many sins. Establish me anew who have been made senseless by transgressions, O Blameless One. Show me a stranger to every torment, and entreat the Master of All. Enable me to attain to the gladness of Heaven together with all the saints. O most ✠ Holy Virgin, hear the voice of your unprofitable servant. Grant me a stream of tears, O Most Pure One, to wash away the defilement of my soul. I bring to you the groanings of my heart unceasingly; beseech the Master to listen. Accept my prayerful service and bear it to the compassionate God! You that are higher than the angels, make me to be above the gloominess of the world. O light-bearing Cloud of Heaven, establish spiritual grace in me. Although stained by sin, I raise my hands and open my lips in praise of you! Deliver me from soul-corrupting wounds, entreating Christ fervently. To Him honor and worship are due, now end ever and unto ages of ages. Amen.

TO THE GUARDIAN ANGEL:

O Holy Angel, keeping guard over my wretched soul and my passionate life: Do not forsake me, a sinner, nor depart from me because of my incontinence. Do not give the evil enemy room to overcome me by force of this mortal body. Strengthen my weak and feeble hand, and set me on the way of salvation. Yes ; O Holy Angel of God, guardian and protector of my wretched soul and body: Forgive me everything by which I have offended you all the days of my life, and even what I have done this past night; protect me during this day, and guard me from every temptation of the enemy, that I may not anger God by any sin. Pray to the Lord for me, that He may confirm me in His fear, and prove me a worthy servant of His goodness. Amen.

TO THE PATRON SAINT:

Pray to God for me, O Saint well-pleasing to God. I fervently entreat you who are the sure help and intercessor for my soul.

OFFICE OF THE HOURS

Said prior to praying the prayer of the hour

O Christ our God, at every season and every hour, in heaven and on earth, Thou art worshipped and glorified. Thou art long-suffering, merciful and compassionate, loving the just and showing mercy to the sinner; calling all to salvation through the promise of blessings to come.

O Lord, in this hour receive our supplications and direct our lives according to Thy commandments.

Sanctify our souls, hallow our bodies, correct our thoughts, and cleanse our minds. Deliver us from all tribulations, evil and distress.

Surround us with Thy holy angels, that guided and guarded by them, we may come to the unity of the faith and to the knowledge of Thine unapproachable glory, for blessed art Thou unto ages of ages. Amen.

Thou who at all times and at every hour, both in Heaven and on earth art worshipped and glorified, O Christ God; long-suffering, plenteous in mercy and compassion; who lovest the just and showest mercy to those who are hardened in sin; who callest all men to salvation through the promise of good things to come. Do Thou, the same Lord, receive also our supplications at this present time, and direct our lives according to Thy commandments.

Sanctify our souls. Purify our bodies. Set aright our minds; cleanse our thoughts; and deliver us from all calamity, wrath, and distress. Surround us with Thy holy angels; that, guided and guarded by their host, we may attain unto the unity of the faith, and unto the comprehension of Thine ineffable glory. For blessed art Thou unto ages of ages. Amen.

FIRST HOUR

"To Thee I pray, O Lord; in the morning Thou hearest my voice!" *Psalm 5*

For millennia before the use of clocks, the hours of the day were reckoned from sunrise. We would say now that the First Hour after sunrise corresponds to about seven o'clock in the morning. Our Church prays and asks God to bless the day at this hour. She particularly beseeches God to guard us from everything which could harm us in body or soul At this time, when the senses are awakening through the material light, she calls for spiritual awakening through the Savior Christ, who is "the true light enlightening every man who comes into the world."

✚ In the name of the Father and of the Son and of the Holy Spirit. Amen.

Come, let us worship!

O Christ our God, at every season and every hour, in heaven and on earth, Thou art worshipped and glorified.

Thou art long-suffering, merciful and compassionate, loving the just and showing mercy to the sinner; calling all to salvation through the promise of blessings to come.

O Lord, in this hour receive our supplications and direct our lives according to Thy commandments.

Sanctify our souls, hallow our bodies, correct our thoughts, cleanse our minds. Deliver us from all tribulations, evil and distress.

Surround us with Thy holy angels, that guided and guarded by them, we may come to the unity of the faith and to the knowledge of Thine unapproachable glory, for Thou art blessed unto ages of ages. Amen.

Heavenly King, Comforter, True Spirit, Who art everywhere and fillest all, Treasury of good things and Giver of life: come and dwell within us, and cleanse us from every impurity, and save our souls, O Good One. *(Bow)*

TRISAGION PRAYERS

✚ Holy God! Holy Mighty! Holy Immortal! Have mercy on us. *(Bow)*

✚ Holy God! Holy Mighty! Holy Immortal! Have mercy on us. *(Bow)*

✚ Holy God! Holy Mighty! Holy Immortal! Have mercy on us. *(Bow)*

✚ Glory to the Father and to the Son and to the Holy Spirit, now and ever and unto ages of ages. Amen. *(Bow)*

THE LORD'S PRAYER

Our Father, Who art in Heaven, hallowed by Thy name. Thy Kingdom come. Thy will be done, on earth as it is in Heaven. Give us this day our daily bread; and forgive us our trespasses, as we forgive those who trespass against us. And lead us not into temptation, but deliver us from evil.

For Thine is the Kingdom, and the power, and the glory of the ✚ Father, and of the Son, and of the Holy Spirit, now and ever and unto ages of ages.

PSALM 5

Give ear to my words, O Lord, consider my meditation.

Hearken unto the voice of my cry, my King, and my God: for unto thee will I pray.

My voice shalt thou hear in the morning, O Lord; in the morning will I direct my prayer unto thee, and will look up.

For thou art not a God that hath pleasure in wickedness: neither shall evil dwell with thee.

The foolish shall not stand in thy sight: thou hatest all workers of iniquity.

Thou shalt destroy them that speak leasing: the Lord will abhor the bloody and deceitful man.

But as for me, I will come into thy house in the multitude of thy mercy: and in thy fear will I worship toward thy holy temple.

Lead me, O Lord, in thy righteousness because of mine enemies; make thy way straight before my face.

For there is no faithfulness in their mouth; their inward part is very wickedness; their throat is an open sepulcher; they flatter with their tongue.

Destroy thou them, O God; let them fall by their own counsels; cast them out in the multitude of their transgressions; for they have rebelled against thee.

But let all those that put their trust in thee rejoice: let them ever shout for joy, because thou defendest them: let them also that love thy name be joyful in thee.

For thou, Lord, wilt bless the righteous; with favor wilt thou compass him as with a shield.

Order my steps in Thy word and so shall no wickedness have dominion over me.

Deliver me from the wrongful dealings of men, and so I shall keep Thy commandments.

Show the light of Thy countenance upon Thy servant and teach me Thy statutes.

Let my mouth be filled with Thy praise, O Lord, that I may sing of Thy glory and honor all the day long.

O Christ the true light, enlightening and sanctifying every man who comes into the world:

Let the light of Thy countenance shine on us, that in it we may behold the ineffable light.

Guide our footsteps aright in keeping Thy commandments.

Through the intercessions of Thine all-pure ✝ Mother and of all the saints. Amen.

PETITION FOR THE CHURCH

The universe offers Thee the God-bearing martyrs as the first-fruits of creation, O Lord and Creator.

Through the ✝ Theotokos and their prayers, establish Thy Church in peace. Through the prayers of our ✝ holy fathers, may the Lord have mercy on us. Amen.

THIRD HOUR

Take not Thy Holy Spirit from me." - *Psalm 51*

At this hour, which corresponds to about nine o'clock in the morning, the believer along with the Church thanks the Heavenly Father for the very rich gift He gave to the Church when at the third hour the Holy Spirit, the Comforter, came down upon the Apostles (Acts 2:16). From that time onward the Holy Spirit ever remains in the Church, guiding, sanctifying and safeguarding it. As we share with every faithful soul this invaluable gift, we thank our God and Father and ask Him never to deprive us of the fruits and graces of the Spirit.

In the name of the ✝ Father and of the Son and of the Holy Spirit. Amen.

Come, let us worship!

O Christ our God, at every season and every hour, in heaven and on earth, Thou art worshipped and glorified.

Thou art long-suffering, merciful and compassionate, loving the just and showing mercy to the sinner; calling all to salvation through the promise of blessings to come.

O Lord, in this hour receive our supplications and direct our lives according to Thy commandments.

Sanctify our souls, hallow our bodies, correct our thoughts, cleanse our minds. Deliver us from all tribulations, evil and distress.

Surround us with Thy holy angels, that guided and guarded by them, we may come to the unity of the faith and to the knowledge of Thine unapproachable glory, for Thou art blessed unto ages of ages. Amen.

Heavenly King, Comforter, True Spirit, Who art everywhere and fillest all, Treasury of good things and Giver of life:

Come and dwell within us, and cleanse us from every impurity, and save our souls, O Good One. *(Bow)*

TRISAGION PRAYERS

✛ Holy God! Holy Mighty! Holy Immortal! Have mercy on us. *(Bow)*

✛ Holy God! Holy Mighty! Holy Immortal! Have mercy on us. *(Bow)*

✛ Holy God! Holy Mighty! Holy Immortal! Have mercy on us. *(Bow)*

✛ Glory to the Father and to the Son and to the Holy Spirit, now and ever and unto ages of ages. Amen. *(Bow)*

THE LORD'S PRAYER

Our Father Who art in heaven, hallowed be Thy name. Thy kingdom come. Thy will be done, on earth as it is in heaven. Give us this day our daily bread. And forgive us our trespasses, as we forgive those who trespass against us. And lead us not into temptation, but deliver us from the evil one. For Thine is the kingdom and the power and the glory, of the Father and of the Son and of the Holy Spirit, now and ever and unto the ages of ages. Amen.

PSALM 25

Unto thee, O Lord, do I lift up my soul.

O my God, I trust in thee: let me not be ashamed, let not mine enemies triumph over me.

Yea, let none that wait on thee be ashamed: let them be ashamed which transgress without cause.

Show me thy ways, O Lord; teach me thy paths.

Lead me in thy truth, and teach me: for thou art the God of my salvation; on thee do I wait all the day.

Remember, O Lord, thy tender mercies and thy loving kindnesses; for they have been ever of old.

Remember not the sins of my youth, nor my transgressions: according to thy mercy remember thou me for thy goodness' sake, O Lord.

Good and upright is the Lord: therefore will he teach sinners in the way.

The meek will he guide in judgment: and the meek will he teach his way.

All the paths of the Lord are mercy and truth unto such as keep his covenant and his testimonies.

For thy name's sake, O Lord, pardon mine iniquity; for it is great.

What man is he that feareth the Lord? Him shall he teach in the way that he shall choose.

His soul shall dwell at ease; and his seed shall inherit the earth. The secret of the Lord is with them that fear him; and he will show them his covenant.

Mine eyes are ever toward the Lord; for he shall pluck my feet out of the net.

Turn thee unto me, and have mercy upon me; for I am desolate and afflicted.

The troubles of my heart are enlarged: O bring thou me out of my distresses.

Look upon mine affliction and my pain; and forgive all my sins.

Consider mine enemies; for they are many; and they hate me with cruel hatred.

O keep my soul, and deliver me: let me not be ashamed; for I put my trust in thee.

Let integrity and uprightness preserve me; for I wait on thee.

Redeem Israel, O God, out of all his troubles.

PRAYER

O Lord, Thou sent down Thy Most Holy Spirit upon Thine apostles at the Third Hour. Take Him not from us, O Good One, but renew Him in us who pray to Thee.

PRAYER OF SAINT BASIL THE GREAT

O Lord our God, Thou hast given Thy peace to men and sent down the gift of Thine all-holy Spirit to Thy disciples and apostles, opening their lips with fiery tongues by Thy power:

Open also my lips and teach me, sinner that I am, how and for what I ought to pray.

Guide my life, O calm Haven of the storm-tossed, and reveal the way in which I should walk.

Renew in me a right spirit and make my mind steady with a governing spirit, so that guided and guarded each day by Thy good Spirit, I may be enabled to practice Thy commandments, always remembering Thy glorious presence which looks upon the deeds men do.

Do not let me be deceived by the corrupting delights of this world, but rather strengthen in me the desire to attain the treasures of the world to come.

For Thou art blessed and praised in all Thy saints, unto ages of ages. Amen.

✠ Through the prayers of our holy fathers, may the Lord have mercy on us. Amen.

SIXTH HOUR

"There they crucified Him .... It was now about the sixth hour." *Luke 23:33, 44*

Now, even more than at other times, we should join in prayer with the Church, for every soul, delivered by Jesus, ought to have a sense of awe and gratitude. At this hour, corresponding to about twelve noon, the divine drama of our Lord's sacrifice began. At Golgotha, "the place of the skull", Jesus was nailed to the Cross like a criminal (Matthew 27:45.; Mark 15:33.; Luke 23:44.). Do not just shudder, considering the terrible image, but rejoice in the infinite love of God. Give Him grateful thanks, for by this, He has wrought our salvation.

✠ In the name of the Father and of the Son and of the Holy Spirit. Amen.

Come, let us worship!

O Christ our God, at every season and every hour, in heaven and on earth, Thou art worshipped and glorified.

Thou art long-suffering, merciful and compassionate, loving the just and showing mercy to the sinner; calling all to salvation through the promise of blessings to come.

O Lord, in this hour receive our supplications and direct our lives according to Thy commandments.

Sanctify our souls, hallow our bodies, correct our thoughts, cleanse our minds. Deliver us from all tribulations, evil and distress.

Surround us with Thy holy angels, that guided and guarded by them, we may come to the unity of the faith and to the knowledge of Thine unapproachable glory, for Thou art blessed unto ages of ages. Amen.

Heavenly King, Comforter, True Spirit, Who art everywhere and fillest all, Treasury of good things and Giver of life: come and dwell within us, and cleanse us from every impurity, and save our souls, O Good One. *(Bow)*

TRISAGION PRAYERS

✚ Holy God! Holy Mighty! Holy Immortal! Have mercy on us. *(Bow)*

✚ Holy God! Holy Mighty! Holy Immortal! Have mercy on us. *(Bow)*

✚ Holy God! Holy Mighty! Holy Immortal! Have mercy on us. *(Bow)*

✚ Glory to the Father and to the Son and to the Holy Spirit, now and ever and unto ages of ages. Amen. *(Bow)*

THE LORD'S PRAYER

Our Father, Who art in Heaven, hallowed by Thy name. Thy Kingdom come. Thy will be done, on earth as it is in Heaven. Give us this day our daily bread; and forgive us our trespasses, as we forgive those who trespass against us. And lead us not into temptation, but deliver us from evil.

For Thine is the Kingdom, and the power, and the glory of the ✚ Father, and of the Son, and of the Holy Spirit, now and ever and unto ages of ages.

PSALM 54

Save me, O God, by thy name, and judge me by thy strength.

Hear my prayer, O God; give ear to the words of my mouth.

For strangers are risen up against me, and oppressors seek after my soul: they have not set God before them.

Behold, God is mine helper: the Lord is with them that uphold my soul. He shall reward evil unto mine enemies: cut them off in thy truth.

I will freely sacrifice unto thee: I will praise thy name, O Lord; for it is good.

For he hath delivered me out of all trouble: and mine eye hath seen his desire upon mine enemies.

PRAYERS

O Christ God, on the sixth day and hour, Thou nailed to the Cross the sin which rebellious Adam committed in paradise. Tear asunder also the bond of our iniquities, and save us!

Thou hast wrought salvation in the midst of the earth, O Christ God.

Thou stretched out Thine all-pure hands upon the Cross; Thou gatherest together all the nations that cry aloud to Thee: Glory to Thee, O Lord!

PRAYER OF SAINT BASIL THE GREAT

O God, Lord of hosts and Maker of all created things, who in Thy great compassion and mercy sent down Thine Only-begotten Son, our Lord Jesus Christ, for the redemption of mankind, and by His precious Cross destroyed the writing of our sins, thereby triumphing over the source and power of darkness:

O Lord and Lover of man, accept also the thanksgiving and fervent prayers of us sinners. Deliver us from every dark and harmful transgression and from all the visible and invisible enemies which seek to destroy us. Nail our flesh to the fear of Thee, and do not incline our hearts to words or thoughts of guile. But wound our souls with Thy love, that ever looking to Thee, and guided by Thee in the light, and beholding Thee, the Light ineffable and everlasting, we may offer ceaseless praise and thanksgiving to Thee:

To the Father who has no beginning, together with Thine only-begotten Son and Thine all-holy, good and life-giving Spirit, now and ever and unto ages of ages. Amen.

Through the prayers of our ✛ holy fathers, may the Lord have mercy on us. Amen.

NINTH HOUR

"And at the ninth hour...Jesus uttered a loud cry and breathed His last" —*Mark 15:34, 37*

At this hour, corresponding to about three o'clock in the afternoon, the drama of our Lord's sacrifice upon the Cross ended as He gave up His spirit to the Heavenly Father. He had promised His Kingdom to the repentant thief (Luke 23:43). Our Church, and with her every faithful soul observing in wonder, gives thanks and prays to the divine Redeemer, singing of these inconceivable and saving events with appropriate hymns. And so the liturgical day is closed with the joy and fulfillment of the Cross of Christ.

In the name of the ✛ Father and of the Son and of the Holy Spirit. Amen.

Come, let us worship!

O Christ our God, at every season and every hour, in heaven and on earth, Thou art worshipped and glorified.

Thou art long-suffering, merciful and compassionate, loving the just and showing mercy to the sinner; calling all to salvation through the promise of blessings to come.

O Lord, in this hour receive our supplications and direct our lives according to Thy commandments.

Sanctify our souls, hallow our bodies, correct our thoughts, cleanse our minds. Deliver us from all tribulations, evil and distress.

Surround us with Thy holy angels, that guided and guarded by them, we may come to the unity of the faith and to the knowledge of Thine unapproachable glory, for blessed art Thou unto ages of ages. Amen.

Heavenly King, Comforter, True Spirit, Who art everywhere and fillest all, Treasury of good things and Giver of life: come and dwell within us, and cleanse us from every impurity, and save our souls, O Good One. *(Bow)*

TRISAGION PRAYERS

✝ Holy God! Holy Mighty! Holy Immortal! Have mercy on us. *(Bow)*

✝ Holy God! Holy Mighty! Holy Immortal! Have mercy on us. *(Bow)*

✝ Holy God! Holy Mighty! Holy Immortal! Have mercy on us. *(Bow)*

✝ Glory to the Father and to the Son and to the Holy Spirit, now and ever and unto ages of ages. Amen. *(Bow)*

THE LORD'S PRAYER

Our Father, Who art in Heaven, hallowed by Thy name. Thy Kingdom come. Thy will be done, on earth as it is in Heaven. Give us this day our daily bread; and forgive us our trespasses, as we forgive those who trespass against us. And lead us not into temptation, but deliver us from evil.

For Thine is the Kingdom, and the power, and the glory of the ✝ Father, and of the Son, and of the Holy Spirit, now and ever and unto ages of ages.

PSALM 84

How amiable are thy tabernacles, O Lord of hosts! My soul length, yea, even fainteth for the courts of the Lord: my heart and my flesh crieth out for the living God.

Yea, the sparrow hath found an house, and the swallow a nest for herself, where she may lay her young, even Thine altars, O Lord of hosts, my King, and my God.

Blessed are they that dwell in thy house: they will be still praising thee.

Blessed is the man whose strength is in thee; in whose heart are the ways of them.

Who passing through the valley of Baca make it a well; the rain also filleth the pools.

They go from strength to strength, every one of them in Zion appeareth before God. O Lord God of hosts, hear my prayer: give ear, O God of Jacob.

Behold, O God our shield, and look upon the face of Thine anointed.

For a day in thy courts is better than a thousand. I had rather be a doorkeeper in the house of my God, than to dwell in the tents of wickedness.

For the Lord God is a sun and shield: the Lord will give grace and glory: no good thing will he withhold from them that walk uprightly.

O Lord of hosts, blessed is the man that trusteth in thee.

PRAYERS

O Christ God, at the ninth hour Thou tasted death in the flesh for our sake: mortify the rebellion of our flesh and save us!

In the midst of two thieves, Thy Cross was revealed as the balance beam of righteousness; For while the one was led down to hell by the burden of his blaspheming, the other was lightened of his sins to the knowledge of things divine.

O Christ our God, glory to Thee!

PRAYER OF SAINT BASIL THE GREAT

O Master and Lord, Jesus Christ our God, who art long-suffering towards our faults and hast brought us even unto this present hour, in which, hanging upon the life-giving Cross, Thou hast opened unto the good thief the way into Paradise, and destroyed death by death:

Be merciful to us, Thy humble and sinful and unworthy servants. For we have sinned and transgressed, and we are not worthy to lift up our eyes and look at the height of heaven, since we have forsaken the path of Thy righteousness and have walked according to the desires of our own hearts.

But we pray Thee of Thy boundless goodness, spare us, O Lord, according to the abundance of Thy mercy, and save us for Thy Holy Name's sake, for our days have been consumed in vanity.

Pluck us from the hand of the adversary, forgive us our sins, and kill our fleshly lusts, that putting off the old man, we may put on the new, and may live for Thee our Master and Protector; and that so, following Thine ordinances, we may attain to eternal rest, in the place where all the joyful dwell.

For Thou, O Christ our God, art indeed the true joy and gladness of those who love Thee, and unto Thee we ascribe glory, together with Thy Father who is without beginning, and Thy most holy, good and life-giving Spirit, now, and ever, and unto the ages of ages. Amen.

✛ Through the prayers of our holy fathers, may the Lord have mercy on us. Amen.

THE EVENING PRAYERS

Guarding yourself with the Sign of the Cross and making bows, say with compunction the Prayer of the Publican:

✝ God be merciful to me a sinner. *(Bow)* Thou hast created me; Lord, have mercy on me. *(Bow)* I have sinned immeasurably; Lord have mercy and forgive me a sinner. *(Bow)*

It is truly meet to bless thee, O ✝ Theotokos, the ever-blessed and most immaculate, and the Mother of our God. More honorable than the cherubim and truly more glorious than the seraphim; thee who without defilement gavest birth to God the Word, the true Mother of God, thee do we magnify. *(Bow)*

✝ Glory to the Father, and to the Son, and to the Holy Spirit. *(Bow)*

Now and ever, and unto the ages of ages. Amen *(Bow)*

Lord, have mercy. Lord, have mercy, Lord, have mercy. *(Bow)*

DISMISSAL

Lord Jesus Christ, Son of God, through the prayers of Thy most pure Mother, by the power of the precious and life-giving Cross, through the prayers of my holy Guardian Angel, and of all the saints, have mercy on me and save me a sinner, for Thou art good and lovest mankind. *(Bow)*

These Entrance Bows are made whenever one enters the church to stand in prayer. Whenever one has finished praying and is about to leave the church, he makes the Departure Bows (in the same manner). And when one is about to leave his home, he also makes the aforementioned bows.

Through the prayers of our holy fathers, Lord Jesus Christ, Son of God, have mercy on us. Amen. *(Bow)*

And making the Sign of the Cross, say the Prayer to the Holy Spirit:

✤ Heavenly King, Comforter, True Spirit, Who art everywhere and fillest all, Treasury of good things and Giver of life: come and dwell within us, and cleanse us from every impurity, and save our souls, O Good One. *(Bow)*

✤ Holy God, Holy Mighty, Holy Immortal, have mercy on us. *(Bow)*
✤ Holy God, Holy Mighty, Holy Immortal, have mercy on us. *(Bow)*
✤ Holy God, Holy Mighty, Holy Immortal, have mercy on us. *(Bow)*

✤ Glory to the Father, and to the Son, and to the Holy Spirit. *(Bow)* Now and ever, and unto the ages of ages. Amen *(Bow)*

✤ Most Holy Trinity, have mercy on us. O Lord, cleanse us from our sins. O Master forgive our iniquities. O Holy One visit and heal our infirmities for Thy name's sake.

Lord, have mercy. *(Three Times)*

✤ Glory to the Father, and to the Son, and to the Holy Spirit. *(Bow)* Now and ever, and unto the ages of ages. Amen *(Bow)*

THE LORD'S PRAYER

People: Our Father, Who art in Heaven, hallowed by Thy name. Thy Kingdom come. Thy will be done, on earth as it is in Heaven. Give us this day our daily bread; and forgive us our trespasses, as we forgive those who trespass against us. And lead us not into temptation, but deliver us from evil.

Priest: For Thine is the Kingdom, and the power, and the glory of the ✤ Father, and of the Son, and of the Holy Spirit, now and ever and unto ages of ages.

If there is no priest, say: Lord Jesus Christ, Son of God, have mercy on us. Amen.

Lord, have mercy. *(Twelve Times)*

✚ Glory to the Father, and to the Son, and to the Holy Spirit. *(Bow)* Now and ever, and unto the ages of ages. Amen *(Bow)*

Come let us worship God our King. *(Bow)* Come let us worship Christ, our King and our God. *(Bow)* Come let us worship and fall down before the very Lord Jesus Christ, our King and our God. *(Bow)*

A PSALM OF REPENTANCE - PSALM 50

Have mercy on me, O God, according to Thy steadfast love; according to Thy abundant mercy, blot out my transgressions.

Wash me thoroughly from my iniquity, and cleanse me from my sin!

For I know my transgressions, and my sin is ever before me.

Against Thee, Thee only, have I sinned, and done that which is evil in Thy sight, so that Thou art justified in Thy sentence and blameless in Thy judgment.

Behold, I was brought forth in iniquity, and in sin did my mother conceive me.

Behold, Thou desirest truth in the inward being; therefore teach me wisdom in my secret heart.

Purge me with hyssop, and I shall be clean; wash me, and I shall be whiter than snow.

Fill me with joy and gladness; let the bones which Thou hast broken rejoice.

Hide Thy face from my sins, and blot out all my iniquities.

Create in me a clean heart, O God, and put a new and right spirit within me.

Cast me not away from Thy presence, and take not Thy Holy Spirit from me.

Restore to me the joy of Thy salvation, and uphold me with a willing spirit.

Then I will teach transgressors Thy ways, and sinners will return to Thee.

Deliver me from blood guiltiness, O God, Thou God of my salvation, and my tongue will sing aloud of Thy deliverance.

Lord, open Thou my lips, and my mouth shall show forth Thy praise.

For Thou hast no delight in sacrifice; were I to give a burnt offering, Thou wouldst not be pleased.

The sacrifice acceptable to God is a broken spirit; a broken and contrite heart, O God Thou wilt not despise.

Do good to Zion in Thy good pleasure; rebuild the walls of Jerusalem.

Then wilt Thou delight in right sacrifices, in burnt offerings and whole burnt offerings; then bulls will be offered on Thy altar.

Having made the Sign of the Cross, recite the Confession of the Faith:

THE CREED

✤ *I believe in one God, the Father, the Almighty, Creator of heaven and earth, and of all things visible and invisible.*

And in one Lord, Jesus Christ, the only begotten Son of God, begotten of the Father before all ages. Light of Light, true God of true God, begotten, not created, of one essence with the Father, through whom all things were made.

For us and for our salvation, He came down from heaven and was incarnate by the Holy Spirit and the Virgin Mary and became man.

He was crucified for us under Pontius Pilate, and He suffered and was buried. On the third day He rose according to the Scriptures.

He ascended into heaven and is seated at the right hand of the Father. He will come again in glory to judge the living and the dead. His kingdom will have no end.

And in the Holy Spirit, the Lord, the Giver of Life, who proceeds from the Father, who together with the Father and the Son is worshiped and glorified, who spoke through the prophets.

In one, holy, catholic, and apostolic Church. I acknowledge one baptism for the forgiveness of sins. I expect the resurrection of the dead. And the life of the age to come. Amen.

ANGELIC SALUTATION TO THE MOST HOLY MOTHER OF GOD:

Virgin Mother of God, rejoice, Mary full of grace, the Lord is with thee. Blessed art thou among women, and blessed is the fruit of thy womb, for thou hast borne Christ the Savior, the Deliverer of our souls. *(Three times with bows)*

KONTAKION FROM THE AKATHIST HYMN TO THE MOTHER OF GOD:

O All-Hymned Mother who didst bear the Word holiest of all holies, accept our present offering, and deliver us from every assault, and rescue from the torment to come all those that cry to thee: Alleluia! *(Three times, with bows to the ground)*

Afterwards, the Prayer of Jesus, three times, with bows.

Lord Jesus Christ, Son of God, have mercy on us. [have mercy on me, a sinner] *(Bow)*

✚ Most Holy Trinity, our God, glory to Thee. *(Bow)*

✚ Most Holy Lady Mother of God, save me thy sinful servant. *(Bow)*

Glory, O Lord, to Thy precious Cross. *(Bow)*

Angel of Christ, my holy Guardian, save me, thy sinful servant. *(Bow)*

Holy Archangels and Angels, pray to God for me a sinner. *(Bow)*

REFRAINS OF SAINTS:

Holy chief Apostles Peter and Paul, pray to God for me a sinner. *(Bow)*

Holy glorious and all-praised Apostle and Evangelist John the Theologian, pray to God for me a sinner. *(Bow)*

Holy glorious Prophet Elijah, pray to God for me a sinner. *(Bow)*

Holy three great Hierarchs Basil the Great, Gregory the Theologian and John Chrysostom, pray to God for me a sinner. *(Bow)*

Hierarch of Christ Nicholas, pray to God for me a sinner. *(Bow)*

Together with these, pray to the saint whose name you bear, and to the saint(s) whose feast day is being celebrated, and likewise any other saints to whom you wish to pray. Afterwards.

✚ All ye saints, pray to God for us *(for me a sinner)*. *(Bow)*

COMMON REFRAINS OF OTHER SAINTS:

To a Martyr: Holy martyr *(Name)*, pray to God for us. *(Bow)*

For a monk: Venerable father *(Name)*, pray to God for us. *(Bow)*

Pray for the health of your parents, relatives, friends and neighbors, saying three times with bows:

Save, O Lord, and have mercy on Thy servant: *(Name)* *(Bow)*

For your spiritual father: Save, O Lord, and have mercy on Thy servant, the priest *[or. abbot, archimandrite]*: *(Name)* *(Bow)*

For the diocesan bishop: Save, O Lord, and have mercy on Thy servant, bishop *[or: archbishop, metropolitan, patriarch]*: *(Name)* *(Bow)*

If you wish to pray more diligently for someone, say this Troparion:

Save, O Lord, and have mercy on Thy servant(s) *(Name)*. *(Bow)* Deliver him *(her, them)* from every tribulation, wrath and need. *(Bow)* From every sickness of soul and body. *(Bow)* Forgive him *(her, them)* every transgression, voluntary and involuntary. *(Bow)* And do whatever is profitable for our souls. *(Bow)*

Then pray for your departed parents, relatives, friends and neighbors, saying three times with bows.

Grant rest, O Lord, to the soul(s) of Thy departed servant(s) *(Name)* *(Bow)*

If you wish to pray more diligently for someone who is departed, say this Troparion:

Grant rest, O Lord, to the soul of Thy departed servant *(Name)* *(Bow)* Forgive and have mercy on him *(her)*, for whatever sins he *(she)* hath humanly committed, as Thou art a God Who lovest mankind. *(Bow)* And deliver him *(her)* from eternal torment. *(Bow)* Make him *(her)* a sharer of the Kingdom of heaven. *(Bow)* And do whatever is profitable for our souls. *(Bow)*

Or this, for several departed.

Grant rest, O Lord, to the souls of Thy departed servants:

(Name) *(Bow)* Forgive and have mercy on them for whatever sins they have humanly committed, as Thou art a God Who

lovest mankind. *(Bow)* And deliver them from eternal torment. *(Bow)* Make them sharers of the Kingdom of heaven. *(Bow)* And do whatever is profitable for our souls. *(Bow)*

Then, during Great Lent say the Prayer of Our Venerable Father Ephraim the Syrian:

O Lord and Master of my life, drive away from me the spirit of despondency, negligence, avarice and idle talk. *(Bow)* But grant me, Thy servant, the spirit of chastity, humility, patience and love, *(Bow)* Yea, O Lord and King, grant me to see mine own transgressions, and not to judge my brother, for blessed art Thou unto the ages. Amen. *(Bow)*

Then, 13 Bows, saying the Jesus Prayer, or these prayers:

Lord Jesus Christ, Son of God, have mercy on me, a sinner. *(Bow)*

God be merciful to me a sinner. *(Bow)*

God, cleanse me of my sins and have mercy on me. *(Bow)*

Thou hast created me; Lord, have mercy on me. *(Bow)*

I have sinned immeasurably; Lord, forgive me. *(Bow)*

Lord Jesus Christ. Son of God, have mercy on me, a sinner. *(Bow)*

God be merciful to me a sinner. *(Bow)*

God, cleanse me of my sins and have mercy on me. *(Bow)*

Thou hast created me; Lord, have mercy on me. *(Bow)*

I have sinned immeasurably; Lord, forgive me. *(Bow)*

God be merciful to me a sinner. *(Bow)*

Thou hast created me; Lord, have mercy on me. *(Bow)*

I have sinned immeasurably; Lord, forgive me. *(Bow)*

Then the prayer is said again:

O Lord and Master of my life, drive away from me the spirit of despondency, negligence, avarice and idle talk. But grant me, Thy servant, the spirit of chastity, humility, patience and love. Yea, O Lord and King, grant me to see mine own transgressions, and not to judge my brother, for blessed art Thou unto the ages. Amen. *(Bow)*

VESPERS

"Let the lifting up of my hands be an evening sacrifice." - *Psalm 141*

From ancient times the Church, under both the old and the new covenants, has ended the day with the setting of the sun, beginning the new day by lighting the lamps of evening. As the day comes to a close, believers, together with the Church, stand before God filled with gratitude. We thank Him for the abundant blessings He has granted to us and to all creation throughout the day just past With the setting of the sun, everything is led towards rest Many psalms of the Old Testament, including 104 and 141, are dedicated to this Hour. Let us pray now, hymning God together with the whole of creation.

✚ In the name of the Father and of the Son and of the Holy Spirit. Amen.

Glory to Thee, our God, Glory to Thee!

Heavenly King, Comforter, True Spirit, Who art everywhere and fillest all, Treasury of good things and Giver of life: come and dwell within us, and cleanse us from every impurity, and save our souls, O Good One. *(Bow)*

TRISAGION PRAYERS

✚ Holy God! Holy Mighty! Holy Immortal! Have mercy on us. *(Bow)*
✚ Holy God! Holy Mighty! Holy Immortal! Have mercy on us. *(Bow)*
✚ Holy God! Holy Mighty! Holy Immortal! Have mercy on us. *(Bow)*

✚ Glory to the Father and to the Son and to the Holy Spirit, now and ever and unto ages of ages. Amen. *(Bow)*

✚ Most Holy Trinity, have mercy on us. O Lord, cleanse us from our sins. O Master pardon our iniquities. O Holy One visit and heal our infirmities for Thy name's sake.

Lord have mercy. Lord have mercy. Lord have mercy. *(Four Times)*

✙ Glory to the Father and to the Son and to the Holy Spirit, now and ever and unto ages of ages. Amen.

THE LORD'S PRAYER

People: Our Father, Who art in Heaven, hallowed by Thy name. Thy Kingdom come. Thy will be done, on earth as it is in Heaven. Give us this day our daily bread; and forgive us our trespasses, as we forgive those who trespass against us. And lead us not into temptation, but deliver us from evil.

Priest: For Thine is the Kingdom, and the power, and the glory of the ✙ Father, and of the Son, and of the Holy Spirit, now and ever and unto ages of ages.
Come, let us worship God our King!

Come, let us worship Christ, our King and our God!

Come, let us worship and fall down before Christ Himself, our King and our God!

PSALM 104

Bless the Lord, O my soul. O Lord my God, thou art very great; thou art clothed with honor and majesty.

Who coverest thyself with light as with a garment: who stretchest out the heavens like a curtain:

Who layeth the beams of his chambers in the waters: who maketh the clouds his chariot: who walketh upon the wings of the wind:

Who maketh his angels spirits; his ministers a flaming fire:

Who laid the foundations of the earth, that it should not be removed forever.

Thou coverest it with the deep as with a garment: the waters stood above the mountains.

At thy rebuke they fled; at the voice of thy thunder they hastened away.

They go up by the mountains; they go down by the valleys unto the place which thou hast founded for them.

Thou hast set a bound that they may not pass over; that they turn not again to cover the earth.

He sendeth the springs into the valleys, which run among the hills; they give drink to every beast of the field: the wild asses quench their thirst

By them shall the fowls of the heaven have their habitation, which sing among the branches.

He watereth the hills from his chambers: the earth is satisfied with the fruit of thy works.

He causeth the grass to grow for the cattle, and herb for the service of man: that he may bring forth food out of the earth;

And wine that maketh glad the heart of man, and oil to make his face to shine, and bread which strengtheneth man's heart.

The trees of the Lord are full of sap; the cedars of Lebanon, which He hath planted;

Where the birds make their nests: as for the stork, the fir trees are her house.

The high hills are a refuge for the wild goats; and the rocks for the conies.

He appointed the moon for seasons: the sun knoweth his going down.

Thou makest darkness, and it is night: wherein all the beasts of the forest do creep forth.

The young lions roar after their prey, and seek their meat from God.

The sun ariseth, they gather themselves together, and lay them down in their dens.

Man goeth forth unto his work and to his labor until the evening.

O Lord, how manifold are thy works! In wisdom hast thou made them all: the earth is full of thy riches.

So is this great and wide sea, wherein are things creeping innumerable, both small and great beasts.

There go the ships: there is that leviathan, whom thou hast made to play therein.

These wait all upon thee; that thou mayest give them their meat in due season.

That thou gives them they gather: thou openest Thine hand, they are filled with good.

Thou hidest thy face, they are troubled: thou takest away their breath, they die, and return to their dust

Thou sendest forth thy spirit, they are created: and thou renews the face of the earth.

The glory of the Lord shall endure forever: the Lord shall rejoice in his works.

He looketh on the earth, and it trembleth: he toucheth the hills, and they smoke.

I will sing unto the Lord as long as I live: I will sing praise to my God while I have my being.

My meditation of him shall be sweet: I will be glad in the Lord.

Let the sinners be consumed out of the earth, and let the wicked be no more. Bless thou the Lord, O my soul. Praise ye the Lord.

PSALM 141

Lord, I cry unto thee: make haste unto me; give ear unto my voice, when I cry unto thee.

Let my prayer be set forth before thee as incense; and the lifting up of my hands as the evening sacrifice.

Set a watch, O Lord, before my mouth; keep the door of my lips.

Incline not my heart to any evil thing, to practice wicked works with men that work iniquity: and let me not eat of their dainties.

Let the righteous smite me; it shall be a kindness: and let him reprove me; it shall be an excellent oil, which shall not break my head: for yet my prayer also shall be in their calamities.

When their judges are overthrown in stony places, they shall hear my words; for they are sweet.

Our bones are scattered at the grave's mouth, as when one cutteth and cleaveth wood upon the earth.

But mine eyes are unto thee, O God the Lord: in thee is my trust; leave not my soul destitute.

Keep me from the snares which they have laid for me, and the gins of the workers of iniquity.

Let the wicked fall into their own nets, whilst that I withal escape.

PSALM 130

Out of the depths have I cried unto thee, O Lord.

Lord, hear my voice: let Thine ears be attentive to the voice of my supplications.

If thou, Lord, shouldest mark iniquities, O Lord, who shall stand?

But there is forgiveness with thee, that thou mayest be feared.

I wait for the Lord, my soul doth wait, and in his word do I hope.

My soul waiteth for the Lord more than they that watch for the morning: I say, more than they that watch for the morning.

Let Israel hope in the Lord: for with the Lord there is mercy, and with him is plenteous redemption.

And he shall redeem Israel from all his iniquities.

O JOYFUL LIGHT

O Joyful Light of the holy glory of the Immortal, Heavenly, Holy, Blessed Father: Jesus Christ!

Now that we have come to the setting of the sun, and see the light of evening, We praise God, ✛ Father, Son, and Holy Spirit. For it is right at all times to worship Thee with voices of praise, O Son of God and Giver of life. Therefore all the world glorifies Thee!

PRAYERS

Enable us, O Lord, to pass this night without sin. Blessed art Thou, O Lord God of our fathers, and praised and glorified be Thy name forever. Amen.

Let Thy mercy, O Lord, be upon us as we have set our hope on Thee.

Blessed art Thou, O Lord, teach me Thy statutes.

Blessed art thou, O Master, give me understanding by thy statutes.

Blessed art thou, O Holy One, enlighten me in thy statutes.

O Lord, thy mercy endureth forever, despise not the work of thy hands.

To Thee belongs worship! To Thee belongs praise! To Thee belongs glory!

To the ✠ Father and to the Son and to the Holy Spirit, now and ever and unto ages of ages. Amen.

PSALM 123

Unto thee lift I up mine eyes, O thou that dwellest in the heavens.

Behold, as the eyes of servants look unto the hand of their masters, and as the eyes of a maiden unto the hand of her mistress; so our eyes wait upon the Lord our God, until that he have mercy upon us.

Have mercy upon us, O Lord, have mercy upon us: for we are exceedingly filled with contempt.

Our soul is exceedingly filled with the scorning of those that are at ease, and with the contempt of the proud.

THE SONG OF SIMEON THE GODBEARER

Lord, now let test Thou Thy servant depart in peace, according to Thy word; For my eyes have seen Thy salvation, which Thou hast prepared before the face of all peoples; A light to enlighten the Gentiles and to be the glory of Thy people Israel.

CONCLUDING PRAYER

All-holy ✚ Trinity, powerful in essence, kingdom undivided, source of all good, be gracious to me, even though I am a sinner. Make my heart firm and wise, and cleanse me of all impurities. Enlighten my mind that I may forever hymn, glorify, and worship Thee saying:

One is Holy, One is the Lord, Jesus Christ, to the glory of God the Father. Amen.

Through the prayers of our holy fathers, may the Lord have mercy on us. Amen.

COMPLINE

Priest: Blessed is our God, always, now and ever, and unto ages of ages!

Reader: Amen! Glory to Thee, our God, glory to Thee! O Heavenly King, the Comforter, the Spirit of Truth, who art everywhere and fillest all things. Treasury of Blessings, and Giver of Life: Come and abide in us, and cleanse us from every impurity, and save our souls, O Good One.

✤ Holy God! Holy Mighty! Holy Immortal! Have mercy on us. *(Bow)*

✤ Holy God! Holy Mighty! Holy Immortal! Have mercy on us. *(Bow)*

✤ Holy God! Holy Mighty! Holy Immortal! Have mercy on us. *(Bow)*

✤ Glory to the Father, and to the Son, and to the Holy Spirit, now and ever, and unto ages of ages. Amen. *(Bow)*

O Most Holy Trinity have mercy on us. Lord, cleanse us from our sins. Master, pardon our transgressions. Holy One, visit and heal our infirmities, for Thy name's sake.

Lord, have mercy! *(Three Times)*

✤ Glory to the Father and to the Son and to the Holy Spirit, now and ever, and unto ages of ages. Amen.

THE LORD'S PRAYER

People: Our Father, Who art in Heaven, hallowed by Thy name. Thy Kingdom come. Thy will be done, on earth as it is in Heaven. Give us this day our daily bread; and forgive us our trespasses, as we forgive those who trespass against us. And lead us not into temptation, but deliver us from evil.

Priest: For Thine is the Kingdom, and the power, and the glory of the ✠ Father, and of the Son, and of the Holy Spirit, now and ever and unto ages of ages.

Reader: Amen! Lord, have mercy! *(Twelve Times)*

✠ Glory to the Father, and to the Son, and to the Holy Spirit, now and ever, and unto ages of ages. *Amen*

Come, let us worship God our King!

Come, let us worship and fall down before Christ, our King and our God!

Come, let us worship and fall down before Christ Himself, our King and our God!

A PSALM OF REPENTANCE - PSALM 50

Have mercy on me, O God, according to Thy steadfast love; according to Thy abundant mercy, blot out my transgressions.

Wash me thoroughly from my iniquity, and cleanse me from my sin!

For I know my transgressions, and my sin is ever before me.

Against Thee, Thee only, have I sinned, and done that which is evil in Thy sight, so that Thou art justified in Thy sentence and blameless in Thy judgment.

Behold, I was brought forth in iniquity, and in sin did my mother conceive me.

Behold, Thou desirest truth in the inward being; therefore teach me wisdom in my secret heart.

Purge me with hyssop, and I shall be clean; wash me, and I shall be whiter than snow.

Fill me with joy and gladness; let the bones which Thou hast broken rejoice.

Hide Thy face from my sins, and blot out all my iniquities. Create in me a clean heart, O God, and put a new and right spirit within me.

Cast me not away from Thy presence, and take not Thy Holy Spirit from me.

Restore to me the joy of Thy salvation, and uphold me with a willing spirit.

Then I will teach transgressors Thy ways, and sinners will return to Thee.

Deliver me from blood guiltiness, O God, Thou God of my salvation, and my tongue will sing aloud of Thy deliverance.

Lord, open Thou my lips, and my mouth shall show forth Thy praise.

For Thou hast no delight in sacrifice; were I to give a burnt offering, Thou wouldst not be pleased.

The sacrifice acceptable to God is a broken spirit; a broken and contrite heart, O God Thou wilt not despise.

Do good to Zion in Thy good pleasure; rebuild the walls of Jerusalem.

Then wilt Thou delight in right sacrifices, in burnt offerings and whole burnt offerings; then bulls will be offered on Thy altar.

PSALM 69

O God, attend to helping me! O Lord, make haste to help me! Let them be put to shame and confusion who seek my life! Let them be turned back in their shame who jeer saying: "Well done! Well done!" May all who seek Thee rejoice and be glad in Thee! May those who love Thy salvation say evermore, "God is great!" But I am poor and needy; hasten to me, O God! Thou art my help and my deliverer; O Lord, do not tarry!

PSALM 142

Hear my prayer, O Lord; give ear to my supplications!

With my own voice I cry to the LORD; with my own voice I beseech the LORD.

Before him I pour out my complaint, tell of my distress in front of him.

When my spirit is faint within me, you know my path. As I go along this path, they have hidden a trap for me.

I look to my right hand to see that there is no one willing to acknowledge me. My escape has perished; no one cares for me.

I cry out to you, LORD, I say, You are my refuge, my portion in the land of the living.

Listen to my cry for help, for I am brought very low. Rescue me from my pursuers, for they are too strong for me.

Lead my soul from prison, that I may give thanks to your name.

Then the righteous shall gather around me because you have been good to me.

THE PRAYERS ON APPROACHING SLEEP

(The following 7 prayers are from the book "Domestic Rule").

FIRST PRAYER OF SAINT MACARIUS THE GREAT - TO GOD THE FATHER

O Eternal God and King of all creation, who has granted me to arrive even at this hour, forgive me the sins that I have committed this day in word, deed and thought. And cleanse, O Lord, my lowly soul from all defilement of flesh and spirit. And grant me, O Lord, to pass the sleep of this night in peace, that when I rise from my humble bed, I may please Thy most holy Name all the days of my life, and may trample down the bodily and bodiless enemies that war against me. Deliver me, O Lord, from vain thoughts and desires which defile me. For Thine is the kingdom, and the power, and the glory, of the Father, and of the Son, and of the Holy Spirit, now and ever, and unto the ages of ages. Amen.

SECOND PRAYER OF SAINT ANTIOCHUS - TO OUR LORD JESUS CHRIST

O Almighty and all-perfect Word of the Father, Jesus Christ, Who in Thy great loving-kindness never departest from Thy servants, but ever abidest in them: O Jesus, good shepherd of all rational sheep, deliver me not to the revolt of the serpent and leave me not to the will of Satan, for the seed of corruption is in me. But do Thou, O adorable and most holy Lord Jesus Christ, guard me as I sleep with Thine unwaning Light, and sanctify me with Thy Holy Spirit, by Whom Thou didst sanctify Thy disciples, and grant me, Thine unworthy servant, the joy of Thy salvation upon my bed. Enlighten my mind with the light of understanding of Thy holy Gospel; my soul with the love of Thy Cross; my heart, with purity of Thy Words; my body, with Thy passionless Passion. Keep my mind with Thy humility, and rouse me in good time to glorify Thee. For most glorious art Thou with the father and with the Holy Spirit, unto the ages. Amen.

THIRD PRAYER, OF THE SAME

O Lord our God, if in anything I have sinned this day, if I have committed any sin in word, deed or thought, forgive me, inasmuch as Thou art good and lovest mankind. Grant me, O God, peaceful and undisturbed sleep. Send me Thy Guardian Angel to protect and preserve me from all evil. For Thou art the Guardian of our souls and bodies, and unto

Thee do we send up glory, to the ✠ Father, and to the Son, and to the Holy Spirit, now and ever, and unto the ages of ages. Amen

FOURTH PRAYER TO ONE'S GUARDIAN ANGEL

O Angel of Christ, my holy Guardian and protector of my soul and body, forgive me all wherein I have sinned before thee in the present day, and from every wile of the inimical foe deliver me, that I may not anger my God by any sin. But pray for me, thy sinful and unworthy servant, that thou mayest show me to be worthy of the goodness and mercy of the All-Holy Trinity, of the Mother of my God, Jesus Christ, and of all the saints: always, now and ever, and unto the ages of ages. Amen.

FIFTH PRAYER – ACCORDING TO THE HOURS OF THE DAY

O Lord, receive me in repentance. O Lord, leave me not. O Lord, lead me not into temptation. O Lord, give me good thoughts. O Lord, grant me tears, the remembrance of death and compunction. O Lord, grant me reconciliation, humility and obedience. O Lord, grant me patience, forbearance and meekness. O Lord, plant in me a good root: the fear of Thee. O Lord, grant me to love Thee with all my mind and soul, and to do Thy will. O Lord, protect me from certain people, from demons and passions and every unseemly thing. O Lord, let it be as Thou willest and as Thou knowest O Lord, may Thy will be done in me – Thine, O Lord, not mine:

Through the prayers of Thy most pure ✠ Mother and of all the saints: For blessed art Thou unto the ages. Amen.

SIXTH PRAYER TO THE MOST HOLY THEOTOKOS

O Good Mother of the good King, Mary, most pure and blessed Mother of God, pour out the mercy of thy Son and our God on my passionate soul, and protect me by thy prayers, that I may pass the remainder of my life without fault and find paradise through thee, ✚ O Virgin Mother of God, who alone art pure and blessed.

SEVENTH PRAYER TO OUR LORD JESUS CHRIST

O Lord Jesus Christ, Son of God, for the sake of Thy most honorable Mother; Thy bodiless Angels; Thy Prophet, Forerunner and Baptist; the divinely inspired Apostles; the radiant and victorious Martyrs; the venerable and God-bearing Fathers; and through the prayers of all the saints: Deliver me from imminent demonic assault. Yea, my Lord and Creator, Who desirest not the death of a sinner, but that he be converted and live: Grant conversion also unto me, wretched and unworthy; pluck me out of the mouth of the pernicious serpent, who is ravening to devour me and to drag me down to hell alive. Yea, my Lord, my consolation, Who wast clothed in corruptible flesh for the sake of me, a wretch: Wrest me from my wretchedness and grant consolation to my wretched soul. Implant in my heart the doing of Thy commandments, the relinquishing of my evil acts and the obtainment of Thy blessedness. For in Thee, O Lord, have I hoped: do Thou save me.

Then say:

In Thee rejoiceth all creation, O thou who art full of grace: the assembly of archangels and the race of men. O hallowed church, mystical paradise, glory of virgins, of whom God, our God before the ages, took flesh and became a child. For He made thy body a throne, and thy womb He made more spacious than the heavens, O Virgin. In Thee rejoiceth all creation, O thou who art full of grace: Glory to thee. *(Bow)*

THE KONTAKION FROM THE AKATHIST HYMN TO THE THEOTOKOS

To thee, our mighty leader in battle, O Theotokos, we thy servants offer hymns of victory and thanksgiving, for we have been delivered from danger. Since thou possesseth power invincible, do thou set us free from every peril, that we may cry to thee: Rejoice! Thou Bride unwedded.

Most glorious and ever-virgin ✚ Mary Theotokos, Mother of Christ our God, accept our prayers, and present them to thy Son and our God, that for thy sake He may save and enlighten our souls.

All my hope I place in thee, O Mother of God; do preserve me under thy shelter. O ✚ Virgin Theotokos, disdain not me, a sinner in need of they help and Thine assistance, for in thee hath my soul hoped: have mercy on me.

Then, if you wish, read a Canon. And after completing the Canon, say: It is truly meet: and a Bow. Or the Zadostoinik for Holy Paschal (the Heirmos of the 9th Ode of the Paschal Canon):

Shine, shine, New Jerusalem, for the glory of the Lord hath shown upon thee. Exult now, and make glad, O Zion; and thou, pure ✚ Mother of God, rejoice in the rising of thy Child. *(Bow)*

This Zadostoinik is said instead of "It is truly meet:" from the Sunday of Pascha until the Leave-taking of the Feast

✚ Glory now and ever: Lord, have mercy. *(Twice)* Lord Bless.

Lord Jesus Christ, Son of God, through the prayers of Thy most pure Mother, and of our venerable and God-bearing fathers, and of all the saints, have mercy on us and save us, for Thou art good and lovest mankind.

And falling down to the ground, say the forgiveness prayer:

Absolve, remit, forgive, O God, my transgressions, voluntary and involuntary, in word and deed, known and unknown, in mind and in thought, by day and by night; forgive me all, for Thou art good and lovest mankind.

Having arisen, say this prayer with bows:

O Lord Who lovest mankind, forgive them that hate and offend us. Do good unto them that do good. Grant all our brethren and our relatives who are far away all petitions which are unto salvation and eternal life. *(Bow)*

Visit them that are sick, and heal them. Free them that are in prison. Be a guide to them that sail the waters. Direct and hasten them that travel. *(Bow)*

Remember, O Lord, our brethren and fellow-believers of the Orthodox faith who are held captive, and deliver them from every evil circumstance. *(Bow)*

Have mercy, O Lord, on them that have given us alms, and have charged us, unworthy though we be, to pray for them; forgive them and have mercy. *(Bow)*

Have mercy, O Lord, on them that labor and them that serve us, and on them that show mercy and that feed us, and grant them all petitions which are unto salvation, and eternal life. *(Bow)*

Remember, O Lord, our fathers and brethren who have gone before us, and make them to dwell where the light of Thy countenance shineth. *(Bow)*

Remember also, O Lord, our lowliness and poverty; enlighten our minds with the light of understanding of Thy Holy Gospel, and direct us in the way of Thy Commandments: through the prayers of Thy ✚ most pure Mother, and of all Thy saints. Amen. *(Bow)*

Finishing these prayers, make the Departure Bows:

God be merciful to me a sinner. *(Bow)* Thou hast created me; Lord, have mercy on me. *(Bow)* I have sinned immeasurably;

Lord, forgive me. *Some say:* have mercy and forgive me a sinner. *(Bow)*

It is truly meet to bless thee, ✠ O Theotokos, the ever-blessed and most immaculate, and the Mother of our God. More honorable than the cherubim and truly more glorious than the seraphim; thee who without defilement gavest birth to God the Word, the true Mother of God, thee do we magnify. *(Bow)*

✠ Glory to the Father, and to the Son, and to the Holy Spirit *(Bow)* now and ever, and unto the ages of ages, Amen. *(Bow)*

Lord, have mercy. *(Twice)* Lord, bless. *(Bow)*

DISMISSAL

Lord Jesus Christ, Son of God, through the prayers of Thy most pure Mother, by the power of the precious and life-giving Cross, through the prayers of my holy Guardian Angel, and of all the saints, have mercy on me and save me a sinner, for Thou art good and lovest mankind. *(Bow)*

And having finished the bows, say this prayer:

All my hope, *(Bow)* I place in thee, O Mother of God; *(Bow)* Do preserve me under thy shelter. *(Bow)*

And rising, again say:

God be merciful to me a sinner. *(Bow)* Thou hast created me; Lord, have mercy on me. *(Bow)* I have sinned immeasurably; Lord, forgive me. *Some say:* have mercy and forgive me a sinner. *(Bow)*

PRAYER OF SAINT JOHN DAMASCENE

SAID WHILE POINTING AT YOUR BED

O Master, Lover of mankind, is this bed to be my coffin, or wilt Thou enlighten my wretched soul with another day? Behold, the coffin layeth before me; behold, death confronteth me. I fear, O Lord, Thy judgment and the endless torments, yet I cease not to do evil. My Lord God, I continually anger Thee, and Thy most pure ✛ Mother, and all the Heavenly Hosts, and my Holy Guardian Angel. I know, O Lord, that I am unworthy of Thy love for mankind, but am worthy of every condemnation and torment. But, O Lord, whether I will it or not, save me. For to save a righteous man is no great thing, and to have mercy on the pure is nothing wonderful, for they are worthy of Thy mercy. But on me, a sinner, show the wonder of Thy mercy; in this reveal Thy love for mankind, lest my wickedness prevail over Thine ineffable goodness and merciful kindness; and order my life as Thou wilt.

This is how we say the prayers in the evening before sleep. Then, these bedtime prayers: When laying down to sleep, make the Sign of the Cross three times, saying the Jesus Prayer. And lying in bed, guard yourself with the Sign of the Cross and say the Prayer to the Precious Cross:

✛ Let God arise and let His enemies be scattered, and let them that hate Him flee from before His face. As smoke vanisheth, so let them vanish; as wax melteth before the fire, so let the demons perish at the presence of them that love God, and who sign themselves with the Sign of the Cross, and who say in gladness: Rejoice, O Cross of the Lord, for Thou drivest away the demons by the power of our Lord Jesus Christ, Who was crucified on thee, Who descended into Hades and trampled on the power of the devil, and gave us His precious and life-giving Cross for the driving away of all enemies. O most precious and life-giving Cross of the Lord, help me together with the most holy Lady ✛ Theotokos, and with all the holy heavenly powers, always, now and ever, and unto the ages of ages. Amen.

My hope is God, my refuge is Christ, and my protection is the Holy Spirit.

DAILY CONFESSION OF SINS

I confess to Thee, my Lord God and Creator, in one Holy Trinity glorified and worshipped, to the ✛ Father, Son, and Holy Spirit, all my sins which I have committed in all the days of my life, and at every hour, at the present time and in the past, day and night, by deed, word, thought, gluttony, drunkenness, secret eating, idle talking, despondency, indolence, contradiction, disobedience, slandering, condemning, negligence, self-love, acquisitiveness, extortion, lying, dishonesty, mercenariness, jealousy, envy, anger, remembrance of wrongs, hatred, bribery: and by all my senses: sight, hearing, smell, taste, touch; and by the rest of my sins, of the soul together with the bodily, through which I have angered Thee, my God and Creator, and dealt unjustly with my neighbor. Sorrowing for these, I stand guilty before Thee, my God, but I have the will to repent. Only help me, O Lord my God, with tears I humbly entreat Thee. Forgive my past sins through Thy compassion, and absolve from all these which I have said in Thy presence, for Thou art good and the Lover of mankind.

When giving thyself up to sleep, say:

Into Thy hands, O Lord Jesus Christ my God, I commit my spirit. Do Thou bless me, do Thou have mercy on me, and grant me life eternal. Amen.

MIDNIGHT SERVICE

"At midnight I will rise to praise Thee." - Psalm 119

When it is possible for us to rise in the middle of the night for prayer, or perhaps impossible for us to sleep so that we turn to prayer, we are able to enter into a long tradition. We find this witnessed to in the Old Testament by the great prophet David. We also find it in the New Testament, there in the jail of Philippi where the apostles Paul and Silas hymned God at midnight, "the prisoners listening to them " (Acts 16:25). This prayer has a particular grace, for while everything is silent and at rest, the soul which loves God rises from her sleep, and together with the heavenly realms, the angels, she sends up her praises and thanksgivings. The saints throughout the ages have had much to tell us concerning the particular blessing the soul feels when it prays at this hour.

✤ In the name of the Father and of the Son and of the Holy Spirit. Amen.

Come, let us worship God our King!

O Christ our God, at every season and every hour, in heaven and on earth, Thou art worshipped and glorified. Thou art long-suffering, merciful and compassionate, loving the just and showing mercy to the sinner; calling all to salvation through the promise of blessings to come.

O Lord, in this hour receive our supplications and direct our lives according to Your commandments. Sanctify our souls, hallow our bodies, correct our thoughts, cleanse our minds. Deliver us from all tribulations, evil and distress. Surround us with Thy holy angels, that guided and guarded by them, we may come to the unity of the faith and to the knowledge of Thine unapproachable glory, for Thou art blessed unto ages of ages. Amen.

✤ Heavenly King, Comforter, True Spirit, Who art everywhere and fillest all, Treasury of good things and Giver of life: come and dwell within us, and cleanse us from every impurity, and save our souls, O Good One. *(Bow)*

TRISAGION PRAYERS

✤ Holy God! Holy Mighty! Holy Immortal! Have mercy on us. *(Bow)*

✚ Holy God! Holy Mighty! Holy Immortal! Have mercy on us. *(Bow)*

✚ Holy God! Holy Mighty! Holy Immortal! Have mercy on us. *(Bow)*

✚ Glory to the Father and to the Son and to the Holy Spirit, now and ever and unto ages of ages. Amen. *(Bow)*

THE LORD'S PRAYER

Our Father Who art in heaven, hallowed be Thy name. Thy kingdom come. Thy will be done, on earth as it is in heaven. Give us this day our daily bread. And forgive us our trespasses, as we forgive those who trespass against us. And lead us not into temptation, but deliver us from the evil one.

For Thine is the kingdom and the power and the glory, of the ✚ Father and of the Son and of the Holy Spirit, now and ever and unto the ages of ages. Amen.

PRAYERS

Now that Thou hast raised me from my bed of sleep, O Lord, enlighten my mind and heart. Open my lips that I may sing to Thee:

Holy, Holy, Holy art Thou, O God! Through the prayers of the ✚ Theotokos, have mercy on us!

Having arisen from sleep, I thank The, All-Holy Trinity, for in Thy great goodness and patience Thou wast not angry with me, Thy sinful and slothful servant, not hast Thou destroyed me with mine iniquities, but hast shown Thy love toward man; and when I was lying in despair, Thou hast raised me up to keep the morning watch and to glorify Thine unconquerable dominion. And now, most holy God and Master, enlighten the eyes of my heart, and open my lips to learn Thy words and to understand Thy commandments; to do Thy will and to sing to Thee in heartfelt confession; to hymn and to glorify Thy most honorable and majestic name, of the ✛ Father and of the Son and of the Holy Spirit, now and ever, and unto the ages of ages. Amen.

PSALM 134

Behold, bless ye the Lord, all *ye* servants of the Lord, which by night stand in the house of the Lord.

Lift up your hands in the sanctuary, and bless the Lord.

The Lord that made heaven and earth bless thee out of Zion.

Through the prayers of our holy fathers, may the Lord have mercy on us. Amen.

COMMON PRAYERS

✠ In the Name of the Father, and of the Son, and of the Holy Spirit. Amen.

Glory to Thee, our God, glory to Thee!

O Heavenly King, the Comforter, the Spirit of Truth who art everywhere and fillest all things. Treasury of Blessings, and Giver of Life: Come and abide in us, and cleanse us from every impurity, and save our souls, O Good One.

✠ Holy God! Holy Mighty! Holy Immortal! Have mercy on us. *(Bow)*
✠ Holy God! Holy Mighty! Holy Immortal! Have mercy on us. *(Bow)*
✠ Holy God! Holy Mighty! Holy Immortal! Have mercy on us. *(Bow)*

✠ Glory to the Father, and to the Son, and to the Holy Spirit, now and ever and unto ages of ages. Amen. *(Bow)*

O most Holy Trinity, have mercy on us. O Lord, cleanse us from our sins. O Master, pardon our transgressions. O Holy One, visit and heal our infirmities, for Thy name's sake. Lord, have mercy. *(Three Times)*

✠ Glory to the Father, and to the Son, and to the Holy Spirit, now and ever and unto ages of ages. Amen.

Our Father, Who art in Heaven, hallowed be Thy name. Thy Kingdom come, Thy will be done, on earth as it is in Heaven. Give us this day our daily bread; and forgive us our trespasses, as we forgive those who trespass against us; and lead us not into temptation, but deliver us from evil.

Lord, have mercy. *(Twelve Times)*

✚ Glory to the Father, and to the Son, and to the Holy Spirit, now and ever and unto ages of ages. Amen.
O come! Let us worship God, our King!

O come! Let us worship and fall down before Christ, our King and our God!

O come! Let us worship and fall down before Christ Himself, our King and our God!

A PSALM OF REPENTANCE - PSALM 50

Have mercy on me, O God, according to Thy steadfast love; according to Thy abundant mercy, blot out my transgressions.

Wash me thoroughly from my iniquity, and cleanse me from my sin!

For I know my transgressions, and my sin is ever before me.

Against Thee, Thee only, have I sinned, and done that which is evil in Thy sight, so that Thou art justified in Thy sentence and blameless in Thy judgment.

Behold, I was brought forth in iniquity, and in sin did my mother conceive me.

Behold, Thou desirest truth in the inward being; therefore teach me wisdom in my secret heart.

Purge me with hyssop, and I shall be clean; wash me, and I shall be whiter than snow.

Fill me with joy and gladness; let the bones which Thou hast broken rejoice.

Hide Thy face from my sins, and blot out all my iniquities.

Create in me a clean heart, O God, and put a new and right spirit within me.

Cast me not away from Thy presence, and take not Thy Holy Spirit from me.

Restore to me the joy of Thy salvation, and uphold me with a willing spirit.

Then I will teach transgressors Thy ways, and sinners will return to Thee.

Deliver me from blood guiltiness, O God, Thou God of my salvation, and my tongue will sing aloud of Thy deliverance.

Lord, open Thou my lips, and my mouth shall show forth Thy praise.

For Thou hast no delight in sacrifice; were I to give a burnt offering, Thou wouldst not be pleased.

The sacrifice acceptable to God is a broken spirit; a broken and contrite heart, O God Thou wilt not despise.

Do good to Zion in Thy good pleasure; rebuild the walls of Jerusalem.

Then wilt Thou delight in right sacrifices, in burnt offerings and whole burnt offerings; then bulls will be offered on Thy altar.

Having made the Sign of the Cross, recite the Confession of the Faith:

THE CREED

✚ *I believe in one God, the Father, the Almighty, Creator of heaven and earth, and of all things visible and invisible.*

And in one Lord, Jesus Christ, the only begotten Son of God, begotten of the Father before all ages. Light of Light, true God of true God, begotten, not created, of one essence with the Father, through whom all things were made.

For us and for our salvation, He came down from heaven and was incarnate by the Holy Spirit and the Virgin Mary and became man.

He was crucified for us under Pontius Pilate, and He suffered and was buried. On the third day He rose according to the Scriptures.

He ascended into heaven and is seated at the right hand of the Father. He will come again in glory to judge the living and the dead. His kingdom will have no end.

And in the Holy Spirit, the Lord, the Giver of Life, who proceeds from the Father, who together with the Father and the Son is worshiped and glorified, who spoke through the prophets.

In one, holy, catholic, and apostolic Church. I acknowledge one baptism for the forgiveness of sins. I expect the resurrection of the dead. And the life of the age to come. Amen.

THE HYMN TO THE THEOTOKOS

It is truly meet to bless you, O ✛ Theotokos, ever blessed and most pure, and the Mother of our God. More honorable than the Cherubim, and more glorious beyond compare than the Seraphim: without defilement you gave birth to God the Word: true ✛ Theotokos, we magnify you.

THE JESUS PRAYER

O Lord Jesus Christ, Son of God, have mercy on me, a sinner.

SPECIAL PRAYERS

BEFORE MEALS:

"The Lord is gracious and merciful. He provides food for those who fear Him." - *Psalm 111:4, 5*
The eyes of all look to You, and You give them their food in due season. You open Your hand and satisfy the desire of every living thing. - *Psalm 145: 15-16*
The poor shall eat and be satisfied; those who seek the Lord shall praise Him. Their hearts shall live forever! - *Psalm 22:26*

Meals can be an important way for Christians to have their Orthodox Faith become part of their daily lives. The Lord chose a meal, the Last Supper, to reveal the nature of His sacrifice for us and our communion with Him (Mark 14:17 ff). Every meal, surrounded by prayer, can become a reminder of His presence with us and our families. As we enjoy His gifts of food and the presence of one another, let us also give thanks for His gifts of life and salvation.

✠ In the name of the Father, and of the Son, and of the Holy Spirit. Amen.

Our Father, Who art in Heaven, hallowed be Thy name. Thy Kingdom come. Thy will be done, on earth as it is in Heaven. Give us this day our daily bread; and forgive us our trespasses, as we forgive those who trespass against us; and lead us not into temptation, but deliver us from evil.

✠ Glory to the Father, and to the Son, and to the Holy Spirit, now and ever and unto ages of ages. Amen.

Lord, have mercy. *(Three Times)*

O Christ our God, bless the food and drink of Thy servants, for Thou art holy always, now and ever and unto ages of ages. Amen.

AFTER MEALS:

We give thanks to Thee, O Christ our God, that Thou hast satisfied us with Thy earthly blessings; deprive us not also of Thy Heavenly Kingdom. As Thou didst enter into the midst of Thy disciples, granting peace; so come into our midst and save us, O Savior!

✦ Glory to the Father, and to the Son, and to the Holy Spirit, now and ever and unto ages of ages. Amen.
Lord, have mercy. *(Three Times)*

Blessed is God, who has mercy on us and nourishes us from His bounteous gifts by His grace and compassion always, now and ever and unto ages of ages. Amen.

BEFORE READING THE SCRIPTURES:

Illumine our hearts, O Master who lovest mankind, with the pure light of Thy divine knowledge. Open the eyes of our mind to the understanding of Thy gospel teachings. Implant also in us the fear of Thy blessed commandments, that trampling down all carnal desires, we may enter upon a spiritual manner of living, both thinking and doing such things as are well-pleasing unto Thee. For Thou art the illumination of our souls and bodies, O Christ our God, and unto Thee we ascribe glory, together with Thy Father, who is from everlasting, and Thine all-holy, good, and life-creating Spirit now and ever and unto ages of ages. Amen.

BEFORE ANY WORK:

O Lord Jesus Christ, the only-begotten Son of the eternal Father, Thou hast said, "With- out me you can do nothing." In faith I embrace Thy words, O Lord, and bow before Thy goodness. Help me to complete the work I am about to begin for Thine own glory: ✦ in the Name of the Father, and of the Son, and of the Holy Spirit. Amen.

AFTER ANY WORK:

Thou, O Christ, art Thyself the fulfillment of all good things! Fill my soul with joy and gladness, and save me, for Thou art all merciful.

FOR THE SICK:

O Christ, who alone art our Defender: Visit and heal Thy suffering servant *(Name)*, delivering him/her from sickness and grievous pains. Raise him/her up that he/she may sing to Thee and praise Thee without ceasing; through the prayers of the ✤ Theotokos, O Thou who alone lovest mankind.

FOR THE DEPARTED:

O God of spirits and of all flesh, who hast trampled down death and overthrown the Devil, and given life to Thy world: Do Thou, the same Lord, give rest to the souls of Thy departed servants in a place of brightness, a place of refreshment, a place of repose, where all sickness, sighing, and sorrow have fled away. Pardon every transgression which they have committed, whether by word or deed or thought. For Thou art a good God and lovest mankind; because there is no man who lives yet does not sin; for Thou only art without sin; Thy righteousness is to all eternity; and Thy word is truth.

For Thou are the Resurrection, the Life, and the Repose of Thy servants who have fallen asleep, O Christ our God, and unto Thee we ascribe glory, together with Thy Father, who is from everlasting, and Thine all-holy, good, and life-creating Spirit, now and ever unto ages of ages. Amen.

PRAYER OF A STUDENT

Christ my Lord, the giver of light and wisdom, who opened the eyes of the blind man and transformed the fishermen into wise heralds and teachers of the gospel through the coming of the Holy Spirit, shine also in my mind the light of the grace of the Holy Spirit. Grant me discernment, understanding and wisdom in learning.

THE JESUS PRAYER

FORMS

Lord Jesus Christ, Son of the living God, have mercy on me, a sinner.
Lord Jesus Christ, Son of God, have mercy on me, a sinner.
Lord Jesus Christ, Son of God, have mercy on me.
Lord Jesus Christ, Son of God, have mercy on us.
Lord Jesus Christ, have mercy on me.
Jesus, have mercy.

REGARDING THE JESUS PRAYER

Theologically, the Jesus Prayer is considered to be the response of the Holy Tradition to the lesson taught by the parable of the Publican and the Pharisee, in which the Pharisee demonstrates the improper way to pray by exclaiming: "Thank you Lord that I am not like the Publican", whereas the Publican prays correctly in humility, saying "Lord have mercy on me, a sinner" *(Luke 18:10-14)*

In the First Epistle to the Thessalonians the Apostle Paul says: "Pray without ceasing." How then, is one to pray unceasingly? By often repeating the Jesus Prayer: "Lord Jesus Christ, Son of God, have mercy on me." By becoming accustomed to this appeal, great consolation and the need to continually make this petition will be felt within, and it will be carried on, as if of itself, within one.

Although in the beginning the enemy of the human race will offer hindrances to this, by causing great weariness, indolence, boredom and overcoming sleep, having withstood all these with the help of God, one will receive peace of soul, spiritual joy, a benevolent disposition towards people, purification of thought, and gratitude towards God. In the very Name of Jesus a great and graceful power is present Many holy and righteous people advise repeating the Jesus Prayer as frequently as possible; without interruption. It is necessary for everyone, whether eating, drinking, sitting, serving, travelling, or in doing anything, to ceaselessly lament: "Lord Jesus Christ, Son of God, have mercy on me" in order that the Name of the Lord Jesus Christ, in descending into the depths of our hearts, may humble the serpent of destruction, and save and enlighten the soul.

'Lord Jesus Christ, Son of God, have mercy on me, a sinner.' Let your attention and instruction be centered on this. Walking, eating, standing in church before the beginning of the service, continue with the prayer; on entering and departing keep this prayer on your lips and within your heart. In such a manner, with the invocation of the Name of God you will find peace, you will attain to purity of spirit and body; and the Holy Spirit, the Origin of all good, will make for Himself a dwelling within you and will guide you in all piety and purity." - *Saint Seraphim of Sarov*

"To more conveniently become accustomed to remembering God, the fervent Christian has a special means, namely, to repeat ceaselessly a brief prayer of two or three words. Mostly this is 'Lord, have mercy.' or 'Lord Jesus Christ, Son of God, have mercy on me, a sinner.' If you have not yet heard of this, then hear it now, and if you have not done it, then begin from this hour to do it." - *Bishop Theophanes the Recluse*

Those who have truly decided to serve the Lord God must train themselves in the remembrance of God and in unceasing prayer to Jesus Christ, saying mentally: "Lord Jesus Christ, Son of God, have mercy on me, a sinner."

Through such activity, and by guarding oneself from distraction, and with the preservation of peace in one's conscience, it is possible to draw near to God and to be united with Him. For, according to the words of St. Isaac the Syrian, "Except for unceasing prayer we cannot draw near to God" - *Saint Seraphim of Sarov*

THE JESUS PRAYER WITH A CHOTKI

Starting with the Cross, make the sign of the cross while saying:

✚ Glory to the Father, and to the Son, and to the Holy Spirit, now and ever, and unto the ages of ages. Amen

On the large bead directly above the Cross say:

✚ Holy God, Holy Mighty, Holy Immortal, have mercy on us.
✚ Holy God, Holy Mighty, Holy Immortal, have mercy on us.
✚ Holy God, Holy Mighty, Holy Immortal, have mercy on us.

Or:

Our Father, Who art in heaven, hallowed be Thy name, Thy Kingdom come, Thy will be done, on earth as it is in heaven. Give us this day our daily bread, and forgive us our debts, as we forgive our debtors. And lead us not into temptation, but deliver us from the evil one. Amen

On the small bead above the large one say:

It is truly meet to bless thee, O ✚ Theotokos, the ever-blessed and most immaculate, and the Mother of our God. More honorable than the cherubim and truly more glorious than the seraphim; thee who without defilement gavest birth to God the Word, the true Mother of God, thee do we magnify

Then starting with the small beads on the body of the Chotki, for each one say the Jesus Prayer:

Lord Jesus Christ, Son of God, have mercy on me, a sinner.

For the larger divider beads on the body of the Chotki say:

✚ Virgin Mother of God, rejoice, Mary full of grace, the Lord is with thee. Blessed art thou among women, and blessed is the fruit of thy womb, for thou hast borne Christ the Savior, the Deliverer of our souls.

Or:

All-Hymned ✚ Mother who didst bear the Word holiest of all holies, accept our present offering, and deliver us from every assault, and rescue from the torment to come all those that cry to thee: Alleluia!

Or:

My most holy Lady ✦ Mother of God, have mercy on me and save me; and help me now in this life, and at the departure of my soul, and in the age to come.

THE WEEKLY CYCLE

SUNDAY:

TONE ONE TROPARION:

When the stone had been sealed by the Jews, while the soldiers were guarding Your most pure Body, You arose on the third day, O Savior, granting life to the world. The powers of heaven therefore cried to You O Giver of Life: Glory to Your Resurrection O Christ! Glory to Your Kingdom! Glory to Your dispensation O Lover of mankind.

TONE ONE KONTAKION:

As God You did rise from the tomb in glory, raising the world with Yourself. Human nature praises You as God for death has vanished. Adam exults O Master! Eve rejoices for she is freed from bondage and cries to You: You are the Giver of Resurrection to all O Christ!

TONE TWO TROPARION:

When You descended to death, O Life Immortal, You did slay hell with the splendor of Your Godhead. And when from the depths You did raise the dead, all the powers of heaven cried out: O Giver of Life, Christ our God, glory to You!

TONE TWO KONTAKION:

Hell became afraid, O almighty Savior, seeing the miracle of Your Resurrection from the tomb! The dead arose! Creation, with Adam, beheld this and rejoiced with You! And the world, O my Savior, praises You forever!

TONE THREE TROPARION:

Let the heavens rejoice, let the earth be glad. For the Lord has shown strength with His arm! He has trampled down death by death! He has become the first born of the dead!

He has delivered us from the depths of hell, and has granted to the world great mercy!

TONE THREE KONTAKION:

On this day You did rise from the tomb, O Merciful One, leading us from the gates of death. On this day Adam exults as Eve rejoices; with the prophets and patriarchs they unceasingly praise the divine majesty of your power!

MONDAY

TROPARION

Supreme Leaders of the Heavenly Hosts, we implore you that by your prayers you will encircle us, unworthy as we are, with the protection of the wings of your immaterial glory, and guard us who fall down I before you and fervently cry: Deliver us from dangers, for you are the commanders of the Powers above.

KONTAKION

Supreme Leaders of God's armies and ministers of the divine glory, princes of the bodiless Angels and guides of men, ask what is good for us and great mercy, as Supreme Leaders of the Bodiless Hosts.

TUESDAY

TROPARION

The memory of the just is celebrated with hymns of praise, but the Lord's testimony is enough for thee, O Forerunner, for thou wast shown to be more wonderful than the Prophets since thou wast granted to baptize in the running waters Him Whom thou didst proclaim. Then having endured great suffering for the Truth, thou didst rejoice to bring, even to those in hell, the good tidings that God Who had appeared in the flesh takes away the sin of the world and grants us the great mercy.

O Prophet of God and Forerunner of Grace, having obtained thy head from the earth as a most sacred rose, we are always receiving healings; for still as of old in the world thou preachest repentance.

WEDNESDAY AND FRIDAY

TROPARION

O Lord, save Thy people and bless Thine inheritance. Grant victory over their enemies to Orthodox Christians, and protect Thy people with Thy Cross.

KONTAKION

O Christ our God, Who wast voluntarily lifted up on the Cross, grant Thy mercies to Thy new people named after Thee. Gladden with Thy power Orthodox Christians and give them victory over their enemies. May they have as an ally that invincible trophy, Thy weapon of peace.

THURSDAY

TROPARION

Holy Apostles, intercede with our merciful God, that He may grant to our souls the forgiveness of our sins.

KONTAKION TO SAINT NICHOLAS

The truth of things revealed thee to thy flock as a rule of faith, a model of meekness, and a teacher of temperance. Therefore thou hast won the heights by humility, riches by poverty. Holy Father Nicholas, intercede with Christ our God that our souls may be saved.

KONIAKION TO THE HOLY APOSTLES

Thou hast taken the firm and divinely inspired Preachers, O Lord, the top Apostles, for the enjoyment of Thy blessings and for repose. For Thou hast accepted their labors and death as above every burnt offering, O Thou Who alone knowest the secrets of our hearts.

SATURDAY

TROPARION FOR ALL SAINTS

Apostles, Martyrs, and Prophets, holy Hierarchs, Saints and Righteous, having fought the good fight and kept the faith you have boldness towards the Savior. Intercede for us with Him, for He is good, we pray, that He may save our souls.

TROPARION FOR THE FAITHFUL DEPARTED

Remember the souls of Thy servants, O Lord, for Thou art good, and insofar as they sinned in this life, forgive them; for no one is sinless but Thee, Who canst also give rest to the departed.

KONTAKION FOR THE FAITHFUL DEPARTED

With the Saints, give rest, O Christ, to the souls of Thy servants, where there is no pain, no sorrow, no sighing, but life everlasting.

KONLAKION FOR MARTYRS

The world offers to Thee, O Lord, as the Father of creation, the God-bearing Martyrs as the first-fruits of nature. By their prayers through the Mother of God keep Thy Church in deep peace, O Most Merciful One.

THE DIVINE LITURGY OF SAINT JOHN CHRYSOSTOM

Priest: Blessed is the kingdom of the ✚ Father and the Son and the Holy Spirit, now and forever and to the ages of ages.

People: *Amen.*

THE GREAT LITANY AND THE ANTIPHONS

Deacon: In peace let us pray to the Lord.

People: *Lord, have mercy.*

Deacon: For the peace of God and the salvation of our souls, let us pray to the Lord.

People: *Lord, have mercy.*

Deacon: For peace of the whole world, for the stability of the holy churches of God, and for the unity of all, let us pray to the Lord.

People: *Lord, have mercy.*

Deacon: For this holy house and for those who enter it with faith, reverence, and the fear of God, let us pray to the Lord.

People: *Lord, have mercy.*

Deacon: For our Archbishop *(Name),* our Bishop *(Name),* the honorable presbyters, the deacons in the service of Christ, and all the clergy and laity, let us pray to the Lord.

People: *Lord, have mercy.*

Deacon: For our country, the president, and all those in public service, let us pray to the Lord.

People: *Lord, have mercy.*

Deacon: For this parish and city, for every city and country, and for the faithful who live in them, let us pray to the Lord.

People: *Lord, have mercy.*

Deacon: For favorable weather, an abundance of the fruits of the earth, and temperate seasons, let us pray to the Lord.

People: *Lord, have mercy.*

Deacon: For travelers by land, sea, and air, for the sick, the suffering, the captives, and for their salvation, let us pray to the Lord.

People: *Lord, have mercy.*

Deacon: For our deliverance from all affliction, wrath, danger, and distress, let us pray to the Lord.

People: *Lord, have mercy.*

Priest: Help us, save us, have mercy upon us, and protect us, O God, by Your grace.

People: *Lord, have mercy.*

Deacon: Remembering our most holy, pure, blessed, and glorious Lady, the ✚ Theotokos and ever virgin Mary, with all the saints, let us commit ourselves and one another and our whole life to Christ our God.

People: *To You, O Lord.*

Priest *(in a low voice):* Lord, our God, whose power is beyond compare, and glory is beyond understanding; whose mercy is boundless, and love for us is ineffable; look upon us and upon this holy house in Your compassion. Grant to us and to those who pray with us Your abundant mercy.

Priest: For to You belong all glory, honor, and worship to the Father and the Son and the Holy Spirit, now and forever and to the ages of ages.

People: *Amen.*

THE FIRST ANTIPHON

(The designated verses from the Psalms are sung with the hymn:)

People: *By the intercessions of the* ✚ *Theotokos, Savior, save us (Three Times)*

Deacon: In peace let us again pray to the Lord.

People: *Lord, have mercy.*

Deacon: Help us, save us, have mercy upon us, and protect us, O God, by Your grace.

People: *Lord, have mercy.*

Deacon: Remembering our most holy, pure, blessed, and glorious Lady, the ✚ Theotokos and ever virgin Mary, with all the saints, let us commit ourselves and one another and our whole life to Christ our God.

People: *To You, O Lord.*

Priest *(in a low voice):* Lord, our God, save Your people and bless Your inheritance; protect the whole body of Your Church; sanctify those who love the beauty of Your house; glorify them in return by Your divine power; and do not forsake us who hope in You.

Priest: For Yours is the dominion, the kingdom, the power, and the glory of the Father and the Son and the Holy Spirit, now and forever and to the ages of ages.

People: *Amen.*

THE SECOND ANTIPHON

(The designated verses from the Psalms are sung with the hymn:)

People: Save us, O Son of God, who is risen from the dead, to You we sing: Alleluia *(Three Times)*

✚ Glory to the Father and the Son and the Holy Spirit, now and forever and to the ages of ages. Amen.

Only begotten Son and Word of God, although immortal You humbled Yourself for our salvation, taking flesh from the holy ✚ Theotokos and ever virgin Mary and, without change, becoming man. Christ, our God, You were crucified but conquered death by death. You are one of the Holy Trinity, glorified with the Father and the Holy Spirit - save us.

Deacon: In peace let us again pray to the Lord.

People: *Lord, have mercy.*

Deacon: Help us, save us, have mercy upon us, and protect us, O God, by Your grace.

People: *Lord, have mercy.*

Deacon: Remembering our most holy, pure, blessed, and glorious Lady, the ✚ Theotokos and ever virgin Mary, with all the saints, let us commit ourselves and one another and our whole life to Christ our God.

People: *To You, O Lord.*

Priest *(in a low voice):* Lord, You have given us grace to offer these common prayers with one heart. You have promised to grant the requests of two or three gathered in Your name. Fulfill now the petitions of Your servants for our benefit, giving us the knowledge of Your truth in this world, and granting us eternal life in the world to come.

Priest: For You are a good and loving God, and to You we give glory, to the Father and the Son and the Holy Spirit, now and forever and to the ages of ages.

People: *Amen.*

THE THIRD ANTIPHON

(The designated verses of the Psalms are sung with the Apolytikion.)

THE ENTRANCE

(While the Apolytikion is sung, the priest carrying the holy Gospel Book comes in procession before the Beautiful Gate and prays in a low voice:)

Priest: Master and Lord our God, You have established in heaven the orders and hosts of angels and archangels to minister to Your glory. Grant that the holy angels may enter with us that together we may serve and glorify Your goodness. For to You belong all glory, honor, and worship to the Father and the Son and the Holy Spirit, now and forever and to the ages of ages. Amen.

(The priest blesses the entrance saying in a low voice:) Blessed is the entrance of Your saints always, now and forever and to the ages of ages. Amen.

(He then raises the holy Gospel Book and says:)

Priest *(Deacon):* Wisdom. Let us be attentive.

People: ✤ *Come, let us worship and bow before Christ. Save us, O Son of God who rose from the dead, to You we sing: Alleluia.*

(The priest enters the sanctuary. The Apolytikion is repeated and the Troparion of the church and the Kontakion of the day are sung.)

THE TRISAGION HYMN

Deacon: Let us pray to the Lord.

People: *Lord, have mercy.*

Priest *(in a low voice):* Holy God, You dwell among Your saints. You are praised by the Seraphim with the three times holy hymn and glorified by the Cherubim and worshiped by all the heavenly powers. You have brought all things out of nothing into being. You have created man and woman in Your image and likeness and adorned them with all the gifts of Your grace. You give wisdom and understanding to the supplicant and do not overlook the sinner but have established repentance as the way of salvation. You have enabled us, Your lowly and unworthy servants, to stand at this hour before the glory of Your holy altar and to offer to You due worship and praise. Master, accept the three times holy hymn also from the lips of us sinners and visit us in Your goodness. Forgive our voluntary and involuntary transgressions, sanctify our souls and bodies, and grant that we may worship and serve You in holiness all the days of our lives, by the intercessions of the holy ✤ Theotokos and of all the saints who have pleased You throughout the ages.

Priest: For You are holy, our God, and to You we give glory, to the ✤ Father and the Son and the Holy Spirit, now and forever.

Deacon: And to the ages of ages.

People: *Amen.*

✤ *Holy God, Holy Mighty, Holy Immortal, have mercy on us* (Bow)

✤ *Holy God, Holy Mighty, Holy Immortal, have mercy on us* (Bow)

✤ *Holy God, Holy Mighty, Holy Immortal, have mercy on us* (Bow)

✤ *Glory to the Father and to the Son and to the Holy Spirit, now and forever and to the ages of ages. Amen. Holy Immortal, have mercy on us.*

Deacon: Again, fervently.

Priest *(turning towards the Prothesis, the priest says in a low voice:)*: Blessed is He who comes in the name of the Lord.

(Then turning towards the holy Table, he says:) Blessed are You on the throne of glory of Your kingdom, seated upon the Cherubim, now and forever and to the ages of ages. Amen.

People: ✝ Holy God, Holy Mighty, Holy Immortal, have mercy on us.

THE EPISTLE

Priest: Let us be attentive.

(The Reader reads the verses from the Psalms.)

Deacon: Wisdom.

Reader: The reading is from *(The name of the book of the New Testament from which the Apostolic reading is taken).*

Deacon: Let us be attentive.

(The Reader reads the designated Apostolic pericope.)

Priest: Peace be with you.

People: *Alleluia. Alleluia. Alleluia.*

Priest *(in a low voice)*: Shine within our hearts, loving Master, the pure light of Your divine knowledge and open the eyes of our minds that we may comprehend the message of your Gospel. Instill in us, also, reverence for Your blessed commandments, so that having conquered sinful desires, we may pursue a spiritual life, thinking and doing all those things that are pleasing to You.

For You, Christ our God, are the light of our souls and bodies, and to You we give glory together with Your Father who is without beginning and Your all holy, good, and life giving Spirit, now and forever and to the ages of ages. Amen.

THE HOLY GOSPEL

Priest: Wisdom. Arise. Let us hear the holy Gospel. Peace be with all.

People: *And with your spirit.*

Deacon: The reading is from the holy Gospel according to *(Name)*. Let us be attentive.

People: *Glory to You, O Lord, glory to You.*

(The Deacon reads the designated pericope of the holy Gospel.)

People: *Glory to You, O Lord, glory to You.*

THE HOMILY

(Following the readings, it is customary for the priest to proclaim the Gospel.)

LITANY OF FERVENT SUPPLICATION

Priest: Let us say with all our soul and with all our mind, let us say:

People: *Lord, have mercy. (One Time)*

Priest: O Lord Almighty, the God of our Fathers, we beseech Thee, hear us and have mercy.

People: *Lord, have mercy. (One Time)*

Priest: Have mercy upon us, O God, according to Thy great goodness, we beseech Thee, hear us and have mercy.

People: *Lord, have mercy. (Three Times)*

Priest: Furthermore we pray for this country, its ruler, *(title and name of the ruler)*, its people, civil authorities and armed forces.

People: *Lord, have mercy. (Three Times)*

Priest: Furthermore we pray for our Most Reverend Bishop *(name of the diocesan bishop, or, if he be an archbishop or metropolitan, mention his rank and name),* and for all the Orthodox bishops.

People: *Lord, have mercy. (Three Times)*

Priest: Furthermore we pray for our brethren: priests, deacons, monks and all other clergy, and for all our brethren in Christ.

People: *Lord, have mercy. (Three Times)*

Priest: Furthermore we pray for the blessed ever-memorable and most holy Orthodox patriarchs, for devout kings and right believing queens, for the blessed founders of this holy church and for all our Orthodox fathers, brethren, and sisters departed from this life before us, and who rest in peace here and everywhere.

People: *Lord, have mercy. (Three Times)*

Priest: Furthermore we pray for mercy, life, peace, health, salvation, visitation, forgiveness and remission of the sins of the servants of God: benefactors, trustees, members and supporters of this holy church.

People: *Lord, have mercy. (Three Times)*

(Here special petitions for the recovery of the sick, or any special needs for individual parishioners are offered.)

Priest: Furthermore we pray for those who bring offerings and do good works in this holy and all-venerable church; for those who labor in its service, for the singers and for the people here present, who await from Thee great and abundant mercy.

People: *Lord, have mercy. (Three Times)*

Priest *(in a low voice):* O Lord our God, accept this fervent supplication from Thy servants, and have mercy upon us according to the multitude of Thy mercies; and send forth Thy compassion upon us and upon all Thy people, who await the rich mercy that cometh from Thee.

Priest: For Thou art a merciful God and lovest mankind, and unto Thee we ascribe glory to the Father, and to the Son, and to the Holy Spirit, now and ever, and unto ages of ages.

LITANY FOR THE DECEASED

(This litany is offered only if there are remembrances for the deceased.)

Priest: Have mercy upon us, O God, according to Thy great mercy, we beseech Thee: hear us, and have mercy.

People: *Lord, have mercy. (Three Times)*

Priest: Furthermore we pray for the repose of the soul(s) of the servant(s) of God *(name(s) of the deceased)*, departed from this life, and that Thou wilt pardon all his *(or her or their)* sins, both voluntary and involuntary.

People: *Lord, have mercy. (Three Times)*

Priest: That the Lord God will establish his *(or her or their)* soul(s) where the just repose.

People: *Lord, have mercy. (Three Times)*

Priest: The mercies of God, the Kingdom of Heaven, and the remission of his *(or her or their)* sins, we ask of Christ, or King Immortal and our God.

People: *Grant this, O Lord.*

Priest: Let us pray to the Lord.

People: *Lord, have mercy. (One Time)*

Priest: O God of spirits, and of all flesh, Who hast trampled down death by death, and overthrown the Devil, and hast bestowed life upon Thy world: do Thou Thyself, O Lord, grant rest to the soul(s) of Thy departed servant(s), *(name(s) of the deceased)*, in a place of brightness, a place of verdure, a place of repose, whence all sickness, sorrow and sighing have fled away.

As the gracious God, Who lovest mankind, pardon every transgression which he *(or she or they)* has *(or have)* committed, whether by word, or deed, or thought. For Thou alone art without sin, and Thy righteousness is to all eternity, and Thy word is truth. For Thou art the Resurrection, and the Life, and the Repose of Thy departed servant(s) *(name-s of the deceased)*. O Christ our God, and unto Thee we ascribe glory, together with Thy Father, Who is from everlasting, and Thine All-Holy, and Good and Life-Giving Spirit, now and ever, and unto ages of ages.

People: *Amen.*

PRAYER OF THE CATECHUMENS

(During the litany of the catechumens, the priest unfolds on the altar table the corporal [antimins], a cloth with a depiction of the burial of Christ.)

Priest: Pray unto the Lord, ye catechumens.

People: *Lord, have mercy.*

Priest: Ye faithful, pray ye for the catechumens, that the Lord may have mercy upon them.

People: *Lord, have mercy.*

Priest: That He may teach them the word of truth;

People: *Lord, have mercy.*

Priest: That He may reveal to them the Gospel of righteousness.

People: *Lord, have mercy.*

Priest: That He may unite them unto His Holy, Universal, and Apostolic Church;
People: *Lord, have mercy.*

Priest: Save them, have mercy upon them, preserve them, and protect them, O God, by Thy grace.

People: *Lord, have mercy.*

Priest: Bow your heads unto the Lord, ye catechumens.

People: *To Thee, O Lord.*

Priest *(in a low voice)*: O Lord, our God, Who dwellest on high and regardest the humble of heart; Who hast sent forth as the salvation of mankind Thine Only-begotten Son and God, our Lord Jesus Christ; look down upon Thy servants, the catechumens, who have bowed their heads before Thee; make them worthy in due season of the laver of regeneration. Unite them to thy Holy, Universal and Apostolic Church, and number them with Thy chosen flock.

Priest: That they also with us may glorify Thy most honorable and majestic Name of the Father, and of the Son and of the Holy Spirit, now and ever and unto ages of ages.

People: *Lord, have mercy.*

DISMISSAL OF THE CATECHUMENS

Priest: All ye catechumens, depart! Depart, ye catechumens! All ye that are catechumens, depart! Let no catechumens remain! But let us who are of the faithful, again and again, in peace pray to the Lord.

People: *Lord, have mercy.*

Priest *(in a low voice)*: We give thanks unto Thee, O Lord God of the Powers, Who hast accounted us worthy to stand even now before Thy holy altar, and to prostrate ourselves before Thy compassion for our sins and errors of the people. Accept our supplications, O God; make us worthy to offer unto Thee prayers and supplications, and bloodless sacrifices for all Thy people. And enable us, whom Thou hast appointed in this Thy ministry, by the power of Thy Holy Spirit, blamelessly and without offense, in the pure testimony of our conscience, to call upon Thee at all times and in every place; that hearing us, Thou mayest show mercy upon us according to the multitude of Thy goodness.

Priest: Help us, save us have mercy upon us and protect us, O god, by Thy grace.

People: *Lord, have mercy.*

Priest: For unto Thee are due all glory, honor, and worship, to the Father, and to the Son and to the Holy Spirit, now and ever, and unto ages of ages.

People: *Amen.*

PRAYER OF THE FAITHFUL

Priest *(in a low voice):* Again, we bow before You and pray to You, O good and loving God. Hear our supplication: cleanse our souls and bodies from every defilement of flesh and spirit, and grant that we may stand before Your holy altar without blame or condemnation. Grant also, O God, progress in life, faith, and spiritual discernment to the faithful who pray with us, so that they may always worship You with reverence and love, partake of Your Holy Mysteries without blame or condemnation, and become worthy of Your heavenly kingdom.

Priest: And grant that always guarded by Your power we may give glory to You, the Father and the Son and the Holy Spirit, now and forever and to the ages of ages.

People: *Amen.*

THE GREAT ENTRANCE

People: *We who mystically represent the Cherubim sing the three times holy hymn to the life giving Trinity. Let us set aside all the cares of life that we may receive the King of all...*

Priest *(While the Cherubic Hymn is being sung, the priest prays in a low voice):* No one bound by worldly desires and pleasures is worthy to approach, draw near or minister to You, the King of glory. To serve You is great and awesome even for the heavenly powers. But because of Your ineffable and immeasurable love for us, You became man without alteration or change.
You have served as our High Priest, and as Lord of all, and have entrusted to us the celebration of this liturgical sacrifice without the shedding of blood. For You alone, Lord our God, rule over all things in heaven and on earth. You are seated on the throne of the Cherubim, the Lord of the Seraphim and the King of Israel.

You alone are holy and dwell among Your saints. You alone are good and ready to hear. Therefore, I implore You, look upon me, Your sinful and unworthy servant, and cleanse my soul and heart from evil consciousness. Enable me by the power of Your Holy Spirit so that, vested with the grace of priesthood, I may stand before Your holy Table and celebrate the mystery of Your holy and pure Body and Your precious Blood.

To You I come with bowed head and pray: do not turn Your face away from me or reject me from among Your children, but make me, Your sinful and unworthy servant, worthy to offer to You these gifts. For You, Christ our God, are the Offerer and the Offered, the One who receives and is distributed, and to You we give glory, together with Your eternal Father and Your holy, good and life giving Spirit, now and forever and to the ages of ages. Amen.

Priest: *(The priest censes and recites in a low voice:)* We who mystically represent the Cherubim sing the three times holy hymn to the life giving Trinity. Let us set aside all the cares of life that we may receive the King of all...

(*On Sundays*) Having beheld the resurrection of Christ, let us worship the holy Lord Jesus, the only Sinless One. We venerate Your cross, O Christ, and we praise and glorify Your holy resurrection. You are our God. We know no other than You, and we call upon Your name. Come, all faithful, let us venerate the holy resurrection of Christ. For behold, through the cross joy has come to all the world. Blessing the Lord always, let us praise His resurrection. For enduring the cross for us, he destroyed death by death.

Have mercy upon me, O God, according to Your great mercy; and according to the multitude of Your compassion, blot out my transgression. Wash me thoroughly from my iniquity, and cleanse me from my sin. For I acknowledge my iniquity, and my sin is ever before me. Against You, You only, have I sinned, and done evil in Your sight, that You may be found just when You speak, and victorious when You are judged.

For behold, I was conceived in iniquity, and in sin my mother bore me. For behold, You have loved truth; You have made known to me the secret and hidden thing of Your wisdom. you shall sprinkle me with hyssop, and I shall be made clean; You shall wash me, and I shall be whiter than snow. Make me to hear joy and gladness, that the afflicted bones may rejoice. Turn Your face away from my sins, and blot out all my iniquities. Create in me a clean heart, O God, and renew a steadfast spirit within me.

Cast me not away from Your presence, and take not Your Holy Spirit from me. Restore to me the joy of Your salvation, and establish me with Your governing Spirit. I shall teach transgressors Your ways, and the ungodly shall turn back to You. Deliver me from blood guiltiness, O God, the God of my salvation, and my tongue shall joyfully declare Your righteousness. Lord, open my lips, and my mouth shall proclaim Your praise.

For if You had desired sacrifice, I would give it; You do not delight in burnt offerings. A sacrifice to God is a broken spirit; God will not despise a broken and a humbled heart. Do good in Your good pleasure to Zion; and let the walls of Jerusalem be built. Then You shall be pleased with a sacrifice of righteousness, with oblation and whole burnt offerings. Then they shall offer bulls on Your altar.

(Then the Great Entrance takes place.)

Deacon: May the Lord God remember all of you in His kingdom, now and forever and to the ages of ages.

People: *Amen.*

(The priest enters the sanctuary, while the people sing the end of the Cherubic Hymn.)

People: *...invisibly escorted by the angelic hosts. Alleluia. Alleluia. Alleluia.*

(After placing the holy gifts on the holy Table, he says the Petitions:)

THE PETITIONS

Deacon: Let us complete our prayer to the Lord.

People: *Lord have mercy.*

Deacon: For the precious gifts here presented, let us pray to the Lord.

People: *Lord have mercy.*

Deacon: For this holy house and for those who enter it with faith, reverence, and the fear of God, let us pray to the Lord.

People: *Lord have mercy.*

Deacon: For our deliverance from all affliction, wrath, danger, and distress, let us pray to the Lord.

People: *Lord have mercy.*

Deacon: Help us, save us, have mercy upon us, and protect us, O God, by Your grace.

People: *Lord have mercy.*

Deacon: For a perfect, holy, peaceful, and sinless day, let us ask the Lord.

People: *Grant this, O Lord.*

Deacon: For an angel of peace, a faithful guide, a guardian of our souls and bodies, let us ask the Lord.

People: *Grant this, O Lord.*

Deacon: For forgiveness and remission of our sins and transgressions, let us ask the Lord.

People: *Grant this, O Lord.*

Deacon: For all that is good and beneficial to our souls, and for peace in the world, let us ask the Lord.

People: *Grant this, O Lord.*

Deacon: For the completion of our lives in peace and repentance, let us ask the Lord.

People: *Grant this, O Lord.*

Deacon: For a Christian end to our lives, peaceful, without shame and suffering, and for a good account before the awesome judgment seat of Christ, let us ask the Lord.

People: *Grant this, O Lord.*

Deacon: Remembering our most holy, pure, blessed, and glorious Lady, the ✚ Theotokos and ever virgin Mary, with all the saints, let us commit ourselves and one another and our whole life to Christ our God.

People: *To You, O Lord.*

THE PRAYER OF THE PROSKOMIDE

Priest *(in a low voice):* Lord, God Almighty, You alone are holy. You accept a sacrifice of praise from those who call upon You with their whole heart. Receive also the prayer of us sinners and let it reach Your holy altar.

Enable us to bring before You gifts and spiritual sacrifices for our sins and for the transgressions of the people. Make us worthy to find grace in Your presence so that our sacrifice may be pleasing to You and that Your good and gracious Spirit may abide with us, with the gifts here presented, and with all Your people.

Priest: Through the mercies of Your only begotten Son with whom You are blessed, together with Your all holy, good, and life giving Spirit, now and forever and to the ages of ages.

People: *Amen.*

Priest: Peace be with all.

People: *And with your spirit.*

Deacon: Let us love one another that with one mind we may confess:

Priest: *(The Priest kisses the holy Gifts saying:)* I love You, Lord, my strength. The Lord is my rock, and my fortress, and my deliverer.

(At this time it is customary for the kiss of peace to be exchanged.)

People: ✛ *Father, Son, and Holy Spirit, Trinity one in essence and inseparable.*

Deacon: Guard the doors. Wisdom. Let us be attentive.

THE CREED

I believe in one God, the Father, the Almighty, Creator of heaven and earth, and of all things visible and invisible.

And in one Lord, Jesus Christ, the only begotten Son of God, begotten of the Father before all ages. Light of Light, true God of true God, begotten, not created, of one essence with the Father, through whom all things were made.
For us and for our salvation, He came down from heaven and was incarnate by the Holy Spirit and the Virgin Mary and became man.

He was crucified for us under Pontius Pilate, and He suffered and was buried. On the third day He rose according to the Scriptures.

He ascended into heaven and is seated at the right hand of the Father. He will come again in glory to judge the living and the dead. His kingdom will have no end.

And in the Holy Spirit, the Lord, the Giver of Life, who proceeds from the Father, who together with the Father and the Son is worshiped and glorified, who spoke through the prophets.

In one, holy, catholic, and apostolic Church. I acknowledge one baptism for the forgiveness of sins. I expect the resurrection of the dead. And the life of the age to come. Amen.

THE HOLY ANAPHORA

Deacon: Let us stand well. Let us stand in awe. Let us be attentive, that we may present the holy offering in peace.

People: *Mercy and peace, a sacrifice of praise.*

Priest: The grace of our Lord Jesus Christ, and the love of God the Father, and the communion of the Holy Spirit, be with all of you.

People: *And with your spirit.*

Priest: Let us lift up our hearts.

People: *We lift them up to the Lord.*

Priest: Let us give thanks to the Lord.

People: *It is proper and right.*

Priest *(in a low voice):* It is proper and right to sing to You, bless You, praise You, thank You and worship You in all places of Your dominion; for You are God ineffable, beyond comprehension, invisible, beyond understanding, existing forever and always the same; You and Your only begotten Son and Your Holy Spirit.

You brought us into being out of nothing, and when we fell, You raised us up again. You did not cease doing everything until You led us to heaven and granted us Your kingdom to come. For all these things we thank You and Your only begotten Son and Your Holy Spirit; for all things that we know and do not know, for blessings seen and unseen that have been bestowed upon us. We also thank You for this liturgy which You are pleased to accept from our hands, even though You are surrounded by thousands of Archangels and tens of thousands of Angels, by the Cherubim and Seraphim, six-winged, many-eyed, soaring with their wings,

Priest: Singing the victory hymn, proclaiming, crying out, and saying:

People: *Holy, holy, holy, Lord Sabaoth, heaven and earth are filled with Your glory. Hosanna in the highest Blessed is He who comes in the name of the Lord. Hosanna to God in the highest*

Priest *(in a low voice):* Together with these blessed powers, merciful Master, we also proclaim and say: You are holy and most holy, You and Your only begotten Son and Your Holy

Spirit. You are holy and most holy, and sublime is Your glory.

You so loved Your world that You gave Your only begotten Son so that whoever believes in Him should not perish, but have eternal life. He came and fulfilled the divine plan for us. On the night when He was delivered up, or rather when He gave Himself up for the life of the world, He took bread in His holy, pure, and blameless hands, gave thanks, blessed, sanctified, broke and gave it to His holy disciples and apostles, saying:

Priest: Take, eat, this is my Body which is broken for you for the forgiveness of sins.

People: *Amen.*

Priest *(in a low voice):* Likewise, after supper, He took the cup, saying:

Drink of it all of you; this is my Blood of the new Covenant which is shed for you and for many for the forgiveness of sins.

People: *Amen.*

Priest *(in a low voice):* Remembering, therefore, this command of the Savior, and all that came to pass for our sake, the cross, the tomb, the resurrection on the third day, the ascension into heaven, the enthronement at the right hand of the Father, and the second, glorious coming, we offer to You these gifts from Your own gifts in all and for all.

People: *We praise You, we bless You, we give thanks to You, and we pray to You, Lord our God.*

Priest *(in a low voice):* Once again we offer to You this spiritual worship without the shedding of blood, and we ask, pray, and entreat You: send down Your Holy Spirit upon us and upon these gifts here presented.

✠ And make this bread the precious Body of Your Christ.

(He blesses the holy Bread.)

Deacon *(in a low voice):* Amen.

Priest *(in a low voice):* ✠ And that which is in this cup the precious Blood of Your Christ.

(He blesses the holy Cup.)

Deacon *(in a low voice):* Amen.

Priest *(in a low voice):* ✠ Changing them by Your Holy Spirit.

(He blesses them both.)

Deacon *(in a low voice):* Amen. Amen. Amen.

Priest *(in a low voice):* So that they may be to those who partake of them for vigilance of soul, forgiveness of sins, communion of Your Holy Spirit, fulfillment of the kingdom of heaven, confidence before You, and not in judgment or condemnation.

Again, we offer this spiritual worship for those who repose in the faith, forefathers, fathers, patriarchs, prophets, apostles, preachers, evangelists, martyrs, confessors, ascetics, and for every righteous spirit made perfect in faith.

Priest: Especially for our most holy, pure, blessed, and glorious Lady, the ✠ Theotokos and ever virgin Mary.

People: It is truly right to bless you, ✠ Theotokos, ever blessed, most pure, and mother of our God. More honorable than the Cherubim, and beyond compare more glorious than the Seraphim, without corruption you gave birth to God the Word. We magnify you, the true ✠ Theotokos.

Priest *(in a low voice):* For Saint John the prophet, forerunner, and baptist; for the holy glorious and most honorable Apostles; for Saint(s) *(Name-s),* whose memory we commemorate today; and for all Your saints, through whose supplications, O God, bless us. Remember also all who have fallen asleep in the hope of resurrection unto eternal life. *(Here the priest commemorates the names of the deceased.)* And grant them rest, our God, where the light of Your countenance shines.

Again, we ask You, Lord, remember all Orthodox bishops who rightly teach the word of Your truth, all presbyters, all deacons in the service of Christ, and everyone in holy orders.

We also offer to You this spiritual worship for the whole world, for the holy, catholic, and apostolic Church, and for those living in purity and holiness. And for all those in public service; permit them, Lord, to serve and govern in peace that through the faithful conduct of their duties we may live peaceful and serene lives in all piety and holiness.

Priest: Above all, remember, Lord, our Archbishop *(Name)* and our Bishop *(Name)*. Grant that they may serve Your holy churches in peace. Keep them safe, honorable, and healthy for many years, rightly teaching the word of Your truth.
Deacon: Remember also, Lord, those whom each of us calls to mind and all Your people.

People: *And all Your people.*

Priest *(in a low voice):* Remember, Lord, the city in which we live, every city and country, and the faithful who dwell in them. Remember, Lord, the travelers, the sick, the suffering, and the captives, granting them protection and salvation. Remember, Lord, those who do charitable work, who serve in Your holy churches, and who care for the poor. And send Your mercy upon us all.

Priest: And grant that with one voice and one heart we may glorify and praise Your most honored and majestic name, of the ✚ Father and the Son and the Holy Spirit, now and forever and to the ages of ages.

People: *Amen.*

Priest: The mercy of our great God and Savior Jesus Christ be with all of you.

People: *And with your spirit.*

Deacon: Having remembered all the saints, let us again in peace pray to the Lord.

People: *Lord have mercy.*

Deacon: For the precious Gifts offered and consecrated, let us pray to the Lord.

People: *Lord have mercy.*

Deacon: That our loving God who has received them at His holy, heavenly, and spiritual altar as an offering of spiritual fragrance, may in return send upon us divine grace and the gift of the Holy Spirit, let us pray.

People: *Lord have mercy.*

Deacon: Having prayed for the unity of faith and for the communion of the Holy Spirit, let us commit ourselves, and one another, and our whole life to Christ our God.

People: *To You, O Lord.*

Priest *(in a low voice):* We entrust to You, loving Master, our whole life and hope, and we ask, pray, and entreat: make us worthy to partake of your heavenly and awesome Mysteries from this holy and spiritual Table with a clear conscience; for the remission of sins, forgiveness of transgressions, communion of the Holy Spirit, inheritance of the kingdom of heaven, confidence before You, and not in judgment or condemnation.

Priest: And make us worthy, Master, with confidence and without fear of condemnation, to dare call You, the heavenly God, Father, and to say:

THE LORD'S PRAYER

People: Our Father, Who art in Heaven, hallowed by Thy name. Thy Kingdom come. Thy will be done, on earth as it is in Heaven. Give us this day our daily bread; and forgive us our trespasses, as we forgive those who trespass against us. And lead us not into temptation, but deliver us from evil.

Priest: For Thine is the Kingdom, and the power, and the glory of the ✚ Father, and of the Son, and of the Holy Spirit, now and ever and unto ages of ages.

People: *Amen.*

Priest: Peace be with all.

People: *And with your spirit.*

Deacon: Let us bow our heads to the Lord.

People: *To You, O Lord.*

Priest *(in a low voice):* We give thanks to You, invisible King. By Your infinite power You created all things and by Your great mercy You brought everything from nothing into being. Master, look down from heaven upon those who have bowed their heads before You; they have bowed not before flesh and blood but before You the awesome God. Therefore, Master, guide the course of our life for our benefit according to the need of each of us. Sail with those who sail; travel with those who travel; and heal the sick, Physician of our souls and bodies.

Priest: By the grace, mercy, and love for us of Your only begotten Son, with whom You are blessed, together with Your all holy, good, and life giving Spirit, now and forever and to the ages of ages.

People: *Amen.*

Priest *(in a low voice):* Lord Jesus Christ, our God, hear us from Your holy dwelling place and from the glorious throne of Your kingdom. You are enthroned on high with the Father and are also invisibly present among us. Come and sanctify us, and let Your pure Body and precious Blood be given to us by Your mighty hand and through us to all Your people.

Deacon: Let us be attentive.

Priest: The holy Gifts for the holy people of God.

People: *One is Holy, one is Lord, Jesus Christ, to the glory of God the Father. Amen.*

HOLY COMMUNION

People: *Praise the Lord from the heavens; praise Him in the highest Alleluia (Three Times)*

(The Communion Hymn changes according to the Feast Day.)

(After the fraction of the sacred Bread, the priest says in a low voice):

Priest: The Lamb of God is broken and distributed; broken but not divided. He is forever eaten yet is never consumed, but He sanctifies those who partake of Him.

(Then the priest places a portion of the sacred Bread in the Cup saying:) The fullness of the Holy Spirit. Amen.

(He then blesses the warm water saying:) Blessed is the fervor of Your saints, now and forever and to the ages of ages. Amen.

(Pouring the water into the Cup crosswise, he says:) The warmth of the Holy Spirit. Amen.

(The Communion Prayers are recited silently by those prepared to receive the holy Mysteries.)

People: I believe and confess, Lord, that You are truly the Christ, the Son of the living God, who came into the world to save sinners, of whom I am the first I also believe that this is truly Your pure Body and that this is truly Your precious Blood. Therefore, I pray to You, have mercy upon me, and forgive my transgressions, voluntary and involuntary, in word and deed, known and unknown. And make me worthy without condemnation to partake of Your pure Mysteries for the forgiveness of sins and for life eternal. Amen.

How shall I, who am unworthy, enter into the splendor of Your saints? If I dare to enter into the bridal chamber, my clothing will accuse me, since it is not a wedding garment; and being bound up, I shall be cast out by the angels. In Your love, Lord, cleanse my soul and save me.

Loving Master, Lord Jesus Christ, my God, let not these holy Gifts be to my condemnation because of my unworthiness, but for the cleansing and sanctification of soul and body and the pledge of the future life and kingdom. It is good for me to cling to God and to place in Him the hope of my salvation. Receive me today, Son of God, as a partaker of Your mystical Supper. I will not reveal Your mystery to Your adversaries. Nor will I give You a kiss as did Judas. But as the thief I confess to You: Lord, remember me in Your kingdom.

(The priest proceeds to receive holy Communion.)

Priest *(in a low voice)*: Behold, I approach Christ, our immortal King and God. - The precious and most holy Body of our Lord, God, and Savior Jesus Christ is given to me *(Name)* the priest, for the forgiveness of my sins and eternal life.

(He then partakes of the sacred Bread.)

The precious and most holy Blood of our Lord, God, and Savior Jesus Christ is given to me *(Name)* the priest, for the forgiveness of my sins and eternal life.

(He then drinks from the holy Cup. Afterwards, he wipes the holy Cup, kisses it, and says:) This has touched my lips, taking away my transgressions and cleansing my sins.

(The priest then transfers the remaining portions of the consecrated Bread into the holy Cup, saying:) Having beheld the resurrection of Christ, let us worship the holy Lord Jesus, the only Sinless One. We venerate Your cross, O Christ, and we praise and glorify Your holy resurrection. You are our God. We know no other than You, and we call upon Your name. Come, all faithful, let us venerate the holy resurrection of Christ. For behold, through the cross joy has come to all the world. Blessing the Lord always, let us praise His resurrection. For enduring the cross for us, He destroyed death by death.

(The priest takes up the holy Cup, proceeds to the Royal Doors, raises the holy Cup, and says:)

Deacon: Approach with the fear of God, faith, and love.

(Those prepared come forth with reverence to receive Holy Communion while the people sing the communion hymn.)

Priest *(When administering Holy Communion, the priest says)*: The servant of God *(Name)* receives the Body and Blood of Christ for forgiveness of sins and eternal life.

(After Communion has been given, the priest blesses the people, saying:)

Priest: Save, O God, Your people and bless Your inheritance.

People: We have seen the true light; we have received the heavenly Spirit; we have found the true faith, worshiping the undivided Trinity, for the Trinity has saved us.

Priest *(Returning to the holy Table, the priest transfers the portions of the Theotokos and of the saints into the holy Cup. Then he does the same for those of the living and the dead saying in a low voice)*: Wash away, Lord, by Your holy Blood, the sins of all those commemorated, through the intercessions of the ✠ Theotokos and all Your saints. Amen.

Be exalted, O God, above the heavens. Let Your glory be over all the earth *(Three Times)*

Priest *(the priest lifts the holy Cup and says in a low voice)*: Blessed is our God.

Always, now and forever and to the ages of ages.

People: Amen.

Let our mouths be filled with Your praise, Lord, that we may sing of Your glory. You have made us worthy to partake of Your holy mysteries. Keep us in Your holiness, that all the day long we may meditate upon Your righteousness. Alleluia. Alleluia. Alleluia.

PRAYER OF THANKSGIVING

Deacon: Let us be attentive. Having partaken of the divine, holy, pure, immortal, heavenly, life giving, and awesome Mysteries of Christ, let us worthily give thanks to the Lord.

People: *Lord, have mercy.*

Deacon: Help us, save us, have mercy upon us, and protect us, O God, by your grace.

People: *Lord, have mercy.*

Deacon: Having prayed for a perfect, holy, peaceful, and sinless day, let us commit ourselves and one another, and our whole life to Christ our God.

People: *To You, O Lord.*

Priest *(in a low voice):* We thank You, loving Master, benefactor of our souls, that on this day You have made us worthy once again of Your heavenly and immortal Mysteries. Direct our ways in the right path, establish us firmly in Your fear, guard our lives, and make our endeavors safe, through the prayers and supplications of the glorious ✚ Theotokos and ever virgin Mary and of all Your saints.

Priest: For You are our sanctification and to You we give glory, to the Father and the Son and the Holy Spirit, now and forever and to the ages of ages.

People: *Amen.*

THE DISMISSAL

Priest: Let us depart in peace.

Deacon: Let us pray to the Lord.

People: *Lord have mercy.*

Priest: Lord, bless those who praise You and sanctify those who trust in You. Save Your people and bless Your inheritance. Protect the whole body of Your Church. Sanctify those who love the beauty of Your house. Glorify them in return by Your divine power, and do not forsake us who hope in You. Grant peace to Your world, to Your churches, to the clergy, to those in public service, to the armed forces, and to all Your people. For every good and perfect gift is from above, coming from You, the Father of lights. To You we give glory, thanksgiving, and worship, to the ✠ Father and the Son and the Holy Spirit, now and forever and to the ages of ages.

People: *Amen.*
Blessed is the name of the Lord, both now and to the ages
(Three Times)

Priest *(The priest proceeds to the Prothesis and prays in a low voice):*
Christ our God, You are the fulfillment of the Law and the prophets. You have fulfilled all the dispensation of the Father. Fill our hearts with joy and gladness always, now and forever and to the ages of ages. Amen.

Deacon: Let us pray to the Lord.

People: *Lord, have mercy (Three Times)*

Father, give the blessing.

Priest: May the blessing of the Lord and His mercy come upon you through His divine grace and love always, now and forever and to the ages of ages.

People: *Amen.*

Priest: Glory to You, O God, our hope, glory to You.

May Christ our true God (who rose from the dead), as a good, loving, and merciful God, have mercy upon us and save us, through the intercessions of His most pure and holy Mother; the power of the precious and life-giving Cross; the protection of the honorable, bodiless powers of heaven; the supplications of the honorable, glorious, prophet, and forerunner John the Baptist; the holy, glorious, and praiseworthy apostles; the holy, glorious, and triumphant martyrs; our holy and God-bearing Fathers *(name of the church)*; the holy and righteous ancestors Joachim and Anna; Saint *(of the day)* whose memory we commemorate today, and all the saints.

People: *Amen.*

Lord, grant long life to him who blesses and sanctifies us.

Priest: Through the prayers of our holy fathers, Lord Jesus Christ, our God, have mercy on us and save us.

People: *Amen.*

Priest *(blessing the people)*: May the holy Trinity protect all of you.

Priest *(Distributing the antidoron, the priest says)*: May the blessing and the mercy of the Lord be with you.

THE ORDER FOR READING
CANONS/AKATHISTS WHEN ALONE

O God, be merciful to me, a sinner. *(Bow)*
O God, cleanse me, a sinner, and have mercy on me. *(Bow)*
Having created me, O Lord, have mercy on me. *(Bow)*
I have sinned immeasurably, O Lord, forgive me. *(Bow)*
My sovereign, most holy Mother of God, save me, a sinner. *(Bow)*
O Angel, my holy Guardian, protect me from all evil. *(Bow)*
Holy Apostle (or martyr, or holy father Name) pray to God for me. *(Bow)*

Through the prayers of our holy fathers, O Lord Jesus Christ, our God, have mercy on us. Amen.

Glory to Thee, our God, glory to Thee.

Heavenly King, Comforter, True Spirit, Who art everywhere and fillest all, Treasury of good things and Giver of life: come and dwell within us, and cleanse us from every impurity, and save our souls, O Good One. *(Bow)*

TRISAGION PRAYERS

✚ Holy God! Holy Mighty! Holy Immortal! Have mercy on us. *(Bow)*
✚ Holy God! Holy Mighty! Holy Immortal! Have mercy on us. *(Bow)*
✚ Holy God! Holy Mighty! Holy Immortal! Have mercy on us. *(Bow)*

✚ Glory to the Father and to the Son and to the Holy Spirit, now and ever and unto ages of ages. Amen. *(Bow)*

THE LORD'S PRAYER

Our Father, Who art in Heaven, hallowed by Thy name. Thy Kingdom come. Thy will be done, on earth as it is in Heaven. Give us this day our daily bread; and forgive us our trespasses, as we forgive those who trespass against us. And lead us not into temptation, but deliver us from evil.

For Thine is the Kingdom, and the power, and the glory of the ✚ Father, and of the Son, and of the Holy Spirit, now and ever and unto ages of ages.

Lord, have mercy. *(Twelve Times)*

✚ Glory to the Father and to the Son and to the Holy Spirit, now and ever and unto ages of ages. Amen. *(Bow)*

O come let us worship God our King.

O come let us worship and fall down before Christ, our King and God.

O come let us worship and fall down before Christ Himself, our King and our God.

A PSALM OF REPENTANCE - PSALM 50

Have mercy on me, O God, according to Thy steadfast love; according to Thy abundant mercy, blot out my transgressions.

Wash me thoroughly from my iniquity, and cleanse me from my sin!

For I know my transgressions, and my sin is ever before me.

Against Thee, Thee only, have I sinned, and done that which is evil in Thy sight, so that Thou art justified in Thy sentence and blameless in Thy judgment.

Behold, I was brought forth in iniquity, and in sin did my mother conceive me.

Behold, Thou desirest truth in the inward being; therefore teach me wisdom in my secret heart.

Purge me with hyssop, and I shall be clean; wash me, and I shall be whiter than snow.

Fill me with joy and gladness; let the bones which Thou hast broken rejoice.

Hide Thy face from my sins, and blot out all my iniquities.

Create in me a clean heart, O God, and put a new and right spirit within me.

Cast me not away from Thy presence, and take not Thy Holy Spirit from me.

Restore to me the joy of Thy salvation, and uphold me with a willing spirit.

Then I will teach transgressors Thy ways, and sinners will return to Thee.

Deliver me from blood guiltiness, O God, Thou God of my salvation, and my tongue will sing aloud of Thy deliverance.

Lord, open Thou my lips, and my mouth shall show forth Thy praise.

For Thou hast no delight in sacrifice; were I to give a burnt offering, Thou wouldst not be pleased.

The sacrifice acceptable to God is a broken spirit; a broken and contrite heart, O God Thou wilt not despise.

Do good to Zion in Thy good pleasure; rebuild the walls of Jerusalem.

Then wilt Thou delight in right sacrifices, in burnt offerings and whole burnt offerings; then bulls will be offered on Thy altar.

THE CREED

✠ *I believe in one God, the Father, the Almighty, Creator of heaven and earth, and of all things visible and invisible. And in one Lord, Jesus Christ, the only begotten Son of God, begotten of the Father before all ages. Light of Light, true God of true God, begotten, not created, of one essence with the Father, through whom all things were made.*

For us and for our salvation, He came down from heaven and was incarnate by the Holy Spirit and the Virgin Mary and became man.

He was crucified for us under Pontius Pilate, and He suffered and was buried. On the third day He rose according to the Scriptures.

He ascended into heaven and is seated at the right hand of the Father. He will come again in glory to judge the living and the dead. His kingdom will have no end.

And in the Holy Spirit, the Lord, the Giver of Life, who proceeds from the Father, who together with the Father and the Son is worshiped and glorified, who spoke through the prophets.

In one, holy, catholic, and apostolic Church. I acknowledge one baptism for the forgiveness of sins. I expect the resurrection of the dead. And the life of the age to come. Amen.

At this point, the Canons and Akathists are read as follows:

A) If one Canon or Akathist is to be read it is read straight through.

B) If more than one Canon is to be read, the first Song of the first Canon is read. If the Refrain before the final or last two Troparia is Glory... Now ... , it is replaced by the Refrain of the Canon and "Most Holy Mother of God, save us" (the latter comes before a Troparion to the Virgin). The first Song of the second Canon is read, beginning with the Refrain (the Eirmios of the first Canon only is read), etc. Glory... and Now... are used only as Refrains before the last two Troparia (or last Troparion) of the final Canon to be read. Then the third Song of the first Canon, beginning with the Eirmos, etc. After the third Song: Lord have mercy *(Three Times)*, Glory... Now... Sedalions. When there are more than one Canon, the Kontakion(s) of the second and any additional ones are read after the Sedalions. Glory... Now... is read before the final verses. Then Songs 4, 5 and 6 are read. After Song 6: Lord, have mercy. *(Three Times)*, Glory... Now ... Kontakion of the first Canon. Then Songs 7, 8 and 9 are read.

C) If an Akathist is read with the Canon(s), it is included after Song 6. All Kontakions of the Canon(s) are read after Song 3 in this case.

After Song 9:

It is meet and right to worship the Father and the Son and the Holy Spirit; the Trinity one in essence and undivided.

✦ *Holy God! Holy Mighty! Holy Immortal! Have mercy on us. (Bow)*

✦ *Holy God! Holy Mighty! Holy Immortal! Have mercy on us. (Bow)*

✦ *Holy God! Holy Mighty! Holy Immortal! Have mercy on us. (Bow)*

✦ Glory to the Father and to the Son and to the Holy Spirit, now and ever and unto ages of ages. Amen. *(Bow)*

THE LORD'S PRAYER

Our Father, Who art in Heaven, hallowed by Thy name. Thy Kingdom come. Thy will be done, on earth as it is in Heaven. Give us this day our daily bread; and forgive us our trespasses, as we forgive those who trespass against us. And lead us not into temptation, but deliver us from evil.

For Thine is the Kingdom, and the power, and the glory of the ✚ Father, and of the Son, and of the Holy Spirit, now and ever and unto ages of ages.

Have mercy on us, O Lord, have mercy on us. For at a loss for any plea we sinners offer to Thee, our Master, this supplication: have mercy on us.

✚ Glory to the Father, and to the Son, and to the Holy Spirit. Lord, have mercy on us, for our trust is in Thee. Be not very angry with us, remember not our sins; but even now regard us, in Thy tender compassion, and deliver us from our enemies. For Thou art our God, and we are Thy people; we are all the work of Thy Hands, and we call on Thy Name.

Both now and ever, and unto the ages of ages. Amen.

Open the door of thy loving-kindness, O blessed ✚ Mother of God, that we who put our hope in thee may not perish. Through thee, may we be delivered from adversities, for thou art the salvation of Christian people.

If no other prayers are to be read, the closing is as follows:

It is meet and right to worship the Father and the Son and the Holy Spirit; the Trinity one in essence and undivided.

Prayer(s) following the Canon (s).

✚ Holy God! Holy Mighty! Holy Immortal! Have mercy on us. *(Bow)*
✚ Holy God! Holy Mighty! Holy Immortal! Have mercy on us. *(Bow)*
✚ Holy God! Holy Mighty! Holy Immortal! Have mercy on us. *(Bow)*
✚ Glory to the Father and to the Son and to the Holy Spirit, now and ever and unto ages of ages. Amen. *(Bow)*

THE LORD'S PRAYER

Our Father, Who art in Heaven, hallowed by Thy name. Thy Kingdom come. Thy will be done, on earth as it is in Heaven. Give us this day our daily bread; and forgive us our trespasses, as we forgive those who trespass against us. And lead us not into temptation, but deliver us from evil.

For Thine is the Kingdom, and the power, and the glory of the ✚ Father, and of the Son, and of the Holy Spirit, now and ever and unto ages of ages.

Lord, have mercy. *(Three Times)*
✚ Glory to the Father and to the Son and to the Holy Spirit, now and ever and unto ages of ages. Amen. *(Bow)*

More honorable than the cherubim and truly more glorious than the seraphim; thee who without defilement gavest birth to God the Word, the true Mother of God, thee do we magnify. *(Bow)*

Through the prayers of our ✚ holy fathers, O Lord Jesus Christ, our God, have mercy on us. Amen.

Those who are preparing for Holy Communion are obliged to read three Canons and one Akathist the evening before. Usually read are the Canons to the Savior, the Mother of God, and the Guardian Angel (in that order), and either an Akathist to the Savior or to the Mother of God. Those who desire to carry out this evening rule of prayer daily receive great spiritual benefit from doing so.

AKATHIST FOR HOLY COMMUNION

KONTAKION I

Chosen Bridegroom of our hearts and souls, through Thine incarnation and death on the cross Thou hast betrothed all mankind to Thyself forever and hast given us as a pledge of eternal life Thy most pure Body and Blood. Lo! At Thy call, I though unworthy, dare to approach Thy divine Table, and struck by its majesty, I cry: Jesus, God of my heart, come and unite me to Thyself forever.

OIKOS I

Thou didst send Thine Angel to the Prophet Isaiah with a live coal from the heavenly altar that his lips might be purified thereby, when, beholding Thee seated upon Thy throne, he was distressed over his impurity. And how shall I, who am defiled in body and soul, dare to approach to partake of Thy divine Mysteries for communion except Thou Thyself purify me from on high? Where fore, I cry out to Thee from the depths of my soul:

Jesus most good, touch also mine impure lips with the fire of Thy grace.

Jesus, burn the thorns of my many transgressions.

Jesus, create in me a clean heart, and renew a right spirit within me.

Jesus, lead my poor soul out of the prison of the passions.

Jesus, destroy in me impure thoughts and evil lusts.

Jesus, guide my feeble steps to the path of Thy commandments.

Jesus, God of my heart, come and unite me to Thyself forever.

KONTAKION II

Greatly desiring to eat a last Passover with Thy disciples before Thy Passion, that in the midst thereof Thou mightiest give them the last and greatest pledge of Thy love, Thou didst send two of them to Jerusalem two days before Thee, that thus they might prepare it. Hence, learning how we, too, ought to prepare ourselves betimes to eat of the divine Passover which is Thy Body and Blood, I cry out to Thee in thanksgiving: Alleluia!

OIKOS II

"Loose thy sandals from off thy feet, for the place whereon thou standest is holy ground" didst Thou say unto Moses from out of the bush which burned yet was not consumed by Thine unseen presence therein. The vessel which containeth Thy Body and Blood is greater and more holy indeed than the unburnt bush, but I am dust, unclean and sold under sin. Wherefore, with humility and faith I cry out to Thee:

Jesus almighty, strip from me the old man and all his works.

Jesus, slay within me the seed of corruption which maketh its nest within me.

Jesus, break Thou the bonds of sin whereby the enemy hath bound me.

Jesus, grant me a humble heart and a broken spirit.

Jesus, drive far from me temptations and occasions for stumbling.

Jesus, establish me in faith and love for Thee.

Jesus, God of my heart, come and unite me to Thyself forever.

KONTAKION III

"Our fathers did eat manna in the wilderness, and are dead. I am the Bread which cometh down from heaven which, if any man eat thereof, he shall live forever. And the Bread which I will give is My Flesh, which I will give for the life of the world," Thou didst say to the Jews that sought to see from Thee a sign from heaven like unto the manna of Moses, And hearing and beholding the fulfillment of the prophecy, we cry out with fear: Alleluia!

OIKOS III

Having risen from the supper, as the holy John doth relate, and girded. Thyself about with a towel, Thou didst wash the feet of the disciples, thereby teaching us that we ought not to approach Thy divine Table in our sins unwashed by tears of repentance. Mindful of my great need for this mystical ablution and of the dearth of tears of my hardened heart, with Peter I cry to Thee:

Jesus all-good, do Thou Thyself wash not only my feet, but my hands and head as well.

Jesus, lay bare before me the abyss of my soul's corruption.

Jesus, open within me the floodgates of heartfelt contrition.

Jesus, bedew me with the drops of Thy loving-kindness.

Jesus, wrap me about with the fear of the judgment and the eternal torments.

Jesus, awaken within me my sleeping conscience and strengthen its voice.

Jesus, God of my heart, come and unite me to Thyself forever.

KONTAKION IV

"Is this not Jesus, the Son of Joseph, Whose father and mother we know? How is it, then, that He saith, I came down from heaven? How can He give His Flesh to eat?" said the Jews among themselves, on hearing Thy most glorious promise to give Thyself as food to the faithful, unable in the hardness of their hearts to believe with humility and cry out to Thee: Alleluia!

OIKOS IV

"Except ye eat the Flesh of the Son of man, and drink His Blood, ye have no life in you," Thou didst tell the Jews that were slow to believe, and this saying was shown to be hard to accept even for certain of Thy disciples that were yet ignorant of the mysteries of the kingdom of heaven. But we, illumined with light of the Gospel and beholding Thy divine glory with face unveiled, cry out to Thee with faith and love:

Jesus, Who canst do everything through the greatness of Thy power and dominion.

Jesus, Who createth and perfecteth more then we can understand and comprehend.

Jesus, Who once rained down manna from heaven as a sign of the present Mystery.

Jesus, Who didst pour forth water from a rock as a prefiguring thereof.

Jesus, Who didst send a cloud of quail as food for the Jews, who .were starving in the wilderness.

Jesus, Who before the very eyes of the doubting Jews didst satisfy five thousand men with five loaves of bread.

Jesus, God of my heart, come and unite me to Thyself forever.

KONTAKION V

While eating Thy supper with Thy disciples, taking bread, and blessing and breaking it, Thou didst give it to them, saying: "Take, eat; this is My Body, which is broken for you for the remission of sins." And thereafter, having given them the Cup, Thou didst say: "Drink ye all of it: this is My Blood of the New Covenant, which is shed for you and for many for the remission of sins." Hearkening to this divine and most sweet voice, with thanksgiving we cry: Alleluia!

OIKOS V

He who eateth My Flesh, and drinketh My Blood, dwelleth in Me, and I in him. He hath eternal life; and I will raise him up at the last day, which is at the resurrection of life and blessedness. Wherefore, seeking to be vouchsafed this longed-for resurrection unto life, from the depths of my soul I cry to Thee:

Jesus, draw nigh unto one that seeketh union to Thee.

Jesus, enter into my inmost parts, into all my members and bones.

Jesus, be Thou a light unto my darkened mind;

Jesus, fill with Thyself the abyss of my heart, which the whole world cannot satisfy.

Jesus, speak through the voice of my conscience; Jesus, stir and guide my will.

Jesus, God of my heart, come and unite me to Thyself forever.

KONTAKION VI

"Verily, verily, I say unto you that one of you shall betray Me," Thou didst say in anguish of spirit to Thy disciples at the supper. And though they were innocent of any intention to betray Thee, each of them asked Thee: "Lord is it I?"

showing thereby the depth of their humility. But what can I say to Thee when I fall and betray Thee seven times a day? Yet keep me Thyself, that I may not fall away utterly, but cry to Thee thankfully: Alleluia!

OIKOS VI

"As the branch cannot bear fruit of itself, except it abide in the vine, no more can ye, except ye abide in Me. He that abideth in Me, and I in him, the same bringeth forth much fruit." Thus, working wonders Thou didst teach Thy beloved disciples on the way to Gethsemane. Therefore, attending to this instruction, and knowing the weakness of my nature without Thy grace, I earnestly cry to Thee:
Jesus, most heavenly Husbandman, do Thou Thyself plant me in Thy life-bearing garden.

Jesus, true vine, graft me to Thyself like a wild branch.

Jesus, unwithering root, fill me with the sap of eternal life.

Jesus, Vanquisher of all mortality, clear away that which hath been dried up within me by the heat of the passions.

Jesus, beautiful goodness, adorn me with the flowers of good thoughts and feelings.

Jesus, rich in mercy, enrich me with the fruits of true repentance and righteousness.

Jesus, God of my heart, come and unite me to Thyself forever.

KONTAKION VII

To the disciple who at the supper leaned upon Thy breast and asked: "Who is it that betrayeth Thee?" Thou didst answer; "He it is to whom I shall give a sop, when I have dipped it." And, having dipped the bread, Thou didst give it to Judas Iscariot, the son of Simon, to move him to repentance. But, being hardened by the spirit of malice, he had no desire to understand his Lord and Master's voice of love. May I be delivered by Thy grace from such hard-heartedness, by crying to Thee: Alleluia!

OIKOS VII

Taking pity on the weakness of our nature, which turneth away from eating human flesh, Thou wast well-pleased to bestow upon us Thine all-pure Body and Blood not manifestly, but under the appearance of Bread and Wine, most wisely ordering the whole matter of our salvation in Thy love for mankind, O Jesus, and accommodating Thy most saving Mysteries to the weakness of our comprehension and senses. Marveling at this condescension of Thy wisdom to the weakness of our nature, I thankfully glorify Thee thus:

Jesus, Who in Thy wisdom and love for mankind arranges all things for our salvation.

Jesus, Who adapts Thy most saving Mysteries to the weakness of our understanding and senses.

Jesus, Who for the assurance of the doubting hast many times manifested Thy very Body and Blood at Thy holy Table, instead of bread and wine.

Jesus, Who hast shown to worthy ministers of the altar the Holy Spirit descending for the consecration of the Gifts;

Jesus, Who instead of unworthy ministers of the altar dost send invisibly Thy holy Angels. for the celebration of the Divine Mysteries.

Jesus, Who through the manifestation of miracles at the holy Table, hast converted to faith many of the impious.

Jesus, God of my heart, come and unite me to Thyself forever.

KONTAKION VIII

And after the sop - that is, after the traitor had eaten the bread Thou gavest him - as the holy John relateth, Satan entered into him. Oh, what a dreadful punishment for unbelief! Oh, how unhappy the lot of the traitor! What should have been for his salvation is turned into death and damnation for him. Bowing reverently before this judgment of Thy righteousness, with fear and trembling I cry to Thee: Alleluia!

OIKOS VIII

"Do this in remembrance of Me," didst Thou say to Thy disciples at the supper, giving them Thy Body under the appearance of Bread, and Thy Blood under the appearance of wine. For as often as we eat this bread, and drink this cup, we show forth Thy death, according to the word of the holy Paul. And now, remembering Thy Passion, with compunction I cry to Thee:

Jesus, Who for the salvation of the world didst give Thyself over voluntarily into the hands of Thine enemies.

Jesus, Who didst not allow legions of angels to appear in Thy defense.

Jesus, Who with a glance and with the crowing of a cock didst convert to repentance an unfaithful disciple.

Jesus, Who didst make no reply to Caiaphas and Pilate who questioned Thee foolishly.

Jesus, Who from the Cross didst ask the Father to forgive the sins of them that crucified Thee.

Jesus, Who in Thy surpassing loving-kindness didst give Thy beloved disciple to Thy Mother as a son.

Jesus, God of my heart, come and unite me to Thyself forever.

KONTAKION IX

"Judas, betrays thou the Son of Man with a kiss?" Thou didst sadly cry out to Thine unfaithful disciple, when he came with a detachment of troops into the Garden of Gethsemane seeking to betray Thee with a kiss. But even these poignant words did not strike his soul, hardened' in evil, with repentance. And, knowing the inconstancy of mine own will, I fear lest at any time I, too, give thee the kiss of Judas, ungrateful as I am. But do Thou Thyself strengthen me by Thy grace, that with the good thief I may ever cry out: Alleluia!

OIKOS IX

I pray that they all may be one, as Thou. Father, art in Me and I in Thee, that they also may be one in Us; that the world may believe." Thus didst Thou exclaim in Thy last great prayer to the Father. Following this, Thy voice most sweet, and trusting in the power of Thy prayer, with faith I cry to Thee:

Jesus, Who gatherest all together as one, unite us all inseparably with Thee and Thy Father.

Jesus, grant that we all abide in oneness of mind, in faith and in love for Thee.

Jesus, Who cannot abide enmity and division, destroy impious heresies and schisms.

Jesus, Who lovest and hast mercy upon all, gather all the lost sheep into one flock.

Jesus, Who guest peace to all, allay the envy and gainsaying among them that call upon Thy name.

Jesus, Who gives me the Communion of Thy very Body and Blood, may I be truly flesh of Thy Flesh and bone of Thy Bones.

Jesus, God of my heart, come and unite me to Thyself forever.

KONTAKION X

By turning water into wine at the wedding supper in Cana of Galilee, Thou didst manifest the first sign of Thy divine power. Then, when about to depart to the Cross as the Bridegroom of souls, Thou didst manifest to them that believe in Thee the last miracle of Thy love, by changing bread into Thy Body; and wine into Thy Blood, and nurtured thereby unto life eternal, I, too, thankfully cry out to Thee: Alleluia!

OIKOS X

On the day of Thy resurrection, accompanying in the guise of a traveler two of Thy disciples on the way to Emmaus, Thou didst instruct them in the mystery of Thy Passion; but their eyes were holden that they should not recognize Thee, though their hearts burned within them at the sweetness of Thy words. But when, bowing to their request, Thou didst go to tarry with them and, and having blessed the Bread, didst give It them, straightway their eyes were opened and they recognized Thee. Like those disciples, I, too, humbly make bold to raise my voice to Thee thus:

Jesus long-suffering, forsake me not on the path of life because of the insufficiency of my faith.

Jesus, teach me, like them, to understand the prophecies concerning Thee and the mystery of union with Thee by grace;

Jesus, warm and inflame my cold heart, as Thou didst those of Thy disciples.

Jesus all-good, abide also with me, for the day of my life is far spent and it is towards evening.

Jesus, grant me to know thee truly in the present breaking of the mystical Bread and in drinking from the Chalice.

Jesus, grant that even I, perceiving the power of Thy love, may become a proclaimer thereof to my brethren.

Jesus, God of my heart, come and unite me to thyself forever.

KONTAKION XI

To him that is victorious hast Thou promised to give to eat of the Tree of Life, which is in the midst of the paradise of God, and of the hidden manna. May I be prepared on earth for this heavenly fare by the Communion of Thy Body and Blood, which as I now unworthily approach, I cry: Alleluia!

OIKOS XI

He that eateth and drinketh unworthily, eateth and drinketh judgment to himself, not discerning the Body and Blood of the Lord, the heaven-rapt Paul doth admonish them that approach for Communion. Wherefore, I, too, fear and tremble at mine unworthiness; yet lest, by separating myself for long from Thy Communion, I fall prey to the noetic wolf, I draw nigh to Thee with such a cry:

Jesus, receive me, as Thou didst receive the publican, the harlot and the thief.

Jesus, disdain not to enter under the roof of my soul, though it is all empty and fallen.

Jesus, open the eyes of my soul, as thou didst open the eyes of the man that was blind from birth.

Jesus, say to me too, as to the paralytic: Arise and walk.

Jesus, stanch the flow of the impure desires of my soul as Thou diet stanch the flux of the woman with an issue of blood.

Jesus, heal the leprosy of my soul and conscience.

Jesus, God of my heart, come and unite me to Thyself forever.

KONTAKION XII

Through the envy of the devil who spoke through the mouth of the serpent, and through the eating of the forbidden fruit, the whole human race lost paradise and was given over to death. But by tasting of Thy most pure Body and Blood all men are again vouchsafed eternal life and rise up to their former state. For the Communion of Thy life-creating Mysteries is an antidote against the venom of the serpent and is the seed of immortality. Wherefore, I thankfully cry out to Thee: Alleluia!

OIKOS XII

Lo! I stand before the vessel which holdeth Thy divine Mysteries, yet I put not away mine evil thoughts. Thine almighty grace alone doth hearten and draw me on. Wherefore casting myself into the -abyss of Thy loving-kindness, I cry out:

Jesus, Who callest all that labor and are heavy laden to rest in Thee, receive me, who labor under the vanity of this world.

Jesus, Who didst come to call not the righteous, but sinners to repentance, absolve me of my sins and passions.
Jesus, Who headset every infirmity and disease, heal Thou the wounds and festering of my soul.

Jesus, Who didst satisfy the hungry, feed me with Thy Body and Blood.

Jesus, Who didst raise the dead, quicken me who have been slain by my sins.

Jesus, Conqueror of hell, rescue me from the jaws of the spirit of malice.

Jesus, God of my heart, come and unite me to Thyself forever.

KONTAKION XIII

O Jesus most sweet and all-compassionate, Who dost ever descend like manna from heaven to nourish our souls and hearts in the mystery of Thy most pure Body and Blood: vouchsafe me to partake uncondemned of Thy Divine Mysteries, that, being healed, nurtured, sanctified and deified by Thee forever, I may thankfully cry: Alleluia!

[Oikos I and Kontakion I are read again.]

OIKOS I

Thou didst send Thine Angel to the Prophet Isaiah with a live coal from the heavenly altar that his lips might be purified thereby, when, beholding Thee seated upon Thy throne, he was distressed over his impurity. And how shall I, who am defiled in body and soul, dare to approach to partake of Thy divine Mysteries for communion except Thou Thyself purify me from on high? Where fore, I cry out to Thee from the depths of my soul:

KONTAKION I

Chosen Bridegroom of our hearts and souls, through Thine incarnation and death on the cross Thou hast betrothed all mankind to Thyself forever and hast given us as a pledge of eternal life Thy most pure Body and Blood. Lo! At Thy call, I though unworthy, dare to approach Thy divine Table, and struck by its majesty, I cry:

Jesus, God of my heart, come and unite me to Thyself forever.

Jesus most good, touch also mine impure lips with the fire of Thy grace.

Jesus, burn the thorns of my many transgressions.

Jesus, create in me a clean heart, and renew a right spirit within me.

Jesus, lead my poor soul out of the prison of the passions.

Jesus, destroy in me impure thoughts and evil lusts.

Jesus, guide my feeble steps to the path of Thy commandments.

Jesus, God of my heart, come and unite me to Thyself forever.

PREPARATORY PRAYERS FOR HOLY COMMUNION

In the Name of the Father and of the Son, and of the Holy Spirit. Amen.

Glory to Thee, our God, glory to Thee.

Heavenly King, Comforter, Spirit of Truth, Who art everywhere present and fillest all things, Treasury of good gifts and Giver of Life, come and abide in us, and cleanse us of all impurity, and save our souls, O Good One.

✚ Holy God! Holy Mighty! Holy Immortal! Have mercy on us. *(Bow)*

✚ Holy God! Holy Mighty! Holy Immortal! Have mercy on us. *(Bow)*

✚ Holy God! Holy Mighty! Holy Immortal! Have mercy on us. *(Bow)*

✚ Glory to the Father and to the Son and to the Holy Spirit, now and ever and unto ages of ages. Amen. *(Bow)*

Most Holy Trinity, have mercy on us. O Lord, wash away our sins. O Master, pardon our transgressions. O Holy One, visit and heal our infirmities for Thy Name's sake.

Lord, have mercy. *(Three Times)*

✚ Glory to the Father and to the Son and to the Holy Spirit, now and ever and unto ages of ages. Amen. *(Bow)*

Our Father, Who art in heaven, hallowed be Thy Name. Thy Kingdom come. Thy will be done, on earth as it is in heaven. Give us this day our daily bread. And forgive us our debts as we forgive our debtors. And lead us not into temptation; but deliver us from the evil one.

For Thine is the kingdom, the power and the glory, of the ✣ Father, and of the Son and of the Holy Spirit, now and ever, and to the ages of ages. Amen.
Lord, have mercy. *(Twelve Times)*

O come let us worship God our King.

O come let us worship and fall down before Christ, our King and God.

O come let us worship and fall down before Christ Himself, our King and our God.

PSALM 23 (22)

The Lord is my shepherd, I shall not want; He makes me lie down in green pastures.

He leads me beside still waters; He restores my soul.

He leads me in the paths of righteousness for His name's sake.

Even though I walk through the valley of the shadow of death, I fear no evil; for Thou art with me; Thy rod and Thy staff, they comfort me.

Thou preparest a table before me in the presence of my enemies; Thou anointest my head with oil, my cup overflows.

Surely goodness and mercy shall follow me all the days of my life; and I shall dwell in the house of the Lord forever.

PSALM 24 (23)

The earth is the Lord's and all that is in it, the world and all who dwell in it He has set it on the seas, and prepared it on the rivers.

Who will ascend the mountain of the Lord, or who will stand in His holy place?

He who has clean hands and a pure heart, who has not set his mind on vanity or sworn deceitfully to his neighbor. He will receive a blessing from the Lord, and mercy from God his Savior.

These are the kind who seek the Lord, who seek the face of the God of Jacob.

Lift up your gates, you princes, and be lifted up, you eternal doors, and the King of Glory will enter.

Who is this King of Glory?

The Lord strong and mighty, the Lord mighty in battle.

Lift up your gates, you princes, and be lifted up, you eternal doors, and the King of Glory will enter.

Who is this King of Glory?

The Lord of Hosts, He is the King of Glory.

PSALM 116 (115)

I believed and so I spoke; but I was deeply humiliated.

I said in my madness: every man is a liar.

What shall I give in return to the Lord for all that He has given me?

I will receive the cup of salvation and call on the Name of the Lord.

I will pay my vows to the Lord in the presence of all His people.

Precious in the sight of the Lord is the death of His Saints.

O Lord, I am Thy slave; I am Thy slave and son of Thy handmaid.

Thou hast broken my bonds asunder.

I will offer Thee the sacrifice of praise, and will pray in the Name of the Lord.

I will pay my vows to the Lord in the presence of all His people, in the courts of the Lord's house, in the midst of thee, O Jerusalem.

PRAYERS

✚ Glory to the Father and to the Son and to the Holy Spirit, now and ever and unto ages of ages. Amen. *(Bow)*

Alleluia, Alleluia, Alleluia. Glory to Thee, O God. *(Three Times)*

Lord, have mercy *(Three Times)*

And then the following prayers:

Overlook my faults, O Lord Who wast born of a Virgin, and purify my heart, and make it a temple for Thy spotless Body and Blood. Let me not be rejected from Thy presence, O Thou Who hast infinitely great mercy.

✚ Glory to the Father, and to the Son, and to the Holy Spirit.

How can I who am unworthy dare to come to the communion of Thy Holy Things? For even if I should dare to approach Thee with those who are worthy, my garment betrays me, for it is not a festal robe, and I shall cause the condemnation of my sinful soul. Cleanse, O Lord, the pollution from my soul, and save me as the Lover of men.

Now and ever, and unto the ages of ages. Amen.

Great is the multitude of my sins, O Mother of God. To thee, O pure one, I flee and implore salvation. Visit my sick and feeble soul and intercede with thy Son and our God, that He may grant me forgiveness for the terrible things I have done, O thou who alone art blessed.

On Holy and Great Thursday the following is read:

When Thy glorious Disciples were enlightened at the Supper by the feet-washing, then impious Judas was darkened with the disease of avarice, and he delivered Thee, the Just Judge, to lawless judges. See, O lover of money, this man through money came to hang himself. Flee the insatiable desire which dared to do such things to the Master. O Lord, Who art good towards all, glory to Thee.

Lord, have mercy. *(Forty Times)*

FIRST PRAYER OF SAINT BASIL THE GREAT

O Sovereign Lord Jesus Christ our God, source of life and immortality, Who art the Author of all creation, visible and invisible, the equally everlasting and co-eternal Son of the eternal Father, Who through the excess of Thy goodness didst in the last days assume our flesh and wast crucified for us, ungrateful and ignorant as we were, and didst cause through Thy own Blood the restoration of our nature which had been marred by sin: O immortal King, accept the repentance even of me a sinner, and incline Thine ear to me and hear my words.

For I have sinned, O Lord, I have sinned against heaven and before Thee, and I am not worthy to gaze on the height of Thy glory; for I have provoked Thy goodness by transgressing Thy commandments and not obeying Thy orders. But Thou, O Lord, in Thy forbearance, patience, and great mercy, hast not given me up to be destroyed with my sins, but Thou awaitest my complete conversion. For Thou, O Lover of men, hast said through Thy Prophet that Thou desirest not the death of the sinner, but that he should return to Thee and live. For Thou dost not will, O Lord, that the work of Thy hands should be destroyed, neither dost Thou delight in the destruction of men, but Thou desirest that all should be saved and come to a knowledge of the Truth.

Therefore, though I am unworthy both of heaven and earth, and even of this transient life, since I have completely succumbed to sin and am a slave to pleasure and have defaced Thy image, yet being Thy work and creation, wretch that I am, even I do not despair of my salvation and dare to draw near to Thy boundless compassion.

So receive even me, O Christ Lover of men, as the harlot, as the thief, as the publican, and as the prodigal; and take from me the heavy burden of my sins, Thou Who takest away the sin of the world, Who healest men's sicknesses, Who callest the weary and heavy laden to Thyself and givest them rest; for Thou camest not to call the righteous but sinners to repentance. And purify me from all defilement of flesh and spirit. Teach me to achieve perfect holiness in the fear of Thee, that with the clear witness of my conscience I may receive the portion of Thy holy Things and be united with Thy holy Body and Blood, and have Thee dwelling and remaining in me with the Father and Thy Holy Spirit. And, O Lord Jesus Christ, my God, let not the communion of Thy immaculate and life-giving Mysteries be to me for condemnation nor let it make me sick in body or soul through my partaking of them unworthily; but grant me till my last breath to receive without condemnation the portion of Thy holy Things, for communion with the Holy Spirit, as a provision for eternal life, and as an acceptable defense at Thy dread tribunal, so that I too with all Thy elect may become a partaker of Thy pure joys which Thou hast prepared for those who love Thee, O Lord, in whom Thou art glorified throughout the ages. Amen.

FIRST PRAYER OF SAINT JOHN CHRYSOSTOM

O Lord my God, I know that I am not worthy or sufficient that Thou shouldest come under the roof of the house of my soul, for all is desolate and fallen, and Thou hast not with me a place fit to lay Thy head. But as from the highest heaven Thou didst humble Thyself for our sake, so now conform Thyself to my humility. And as Thou didst consent to lie in a cave and in a manger of dumb beasts, so also consent to lie in the manger of my unspiritual soul and to enter my defiled body.

And as Thou didst not disdain to enter and dine with sinners in the house of Simon the Leper, so consent also to enter the house of my humble soul which is leprous and sinful. And as Thou didst not reject the woman, who was a harlot and a sinner like me, when she approached and touched Thee, so also be compassionate with me, a sinner, as I approach and touch Thee, and let the live coal of Thy most holy Body and precious Blood be for the sanctification and enlightenment and strengthening of my humble soul and body, for a relief from the burden of my many sins, for a protection from all diabolical practices, for a restraint and a check on my evil and wicked way of life, for the mortification of passions, for the keeping of Thy commandments, for an increase of Thy divine grace, and for the advancement of Thy Kingdom.

For it is not insolently that I draw near to Thee, O Christ my God, but as taking courage from Thy unspeakable goodness, and that I may not by long abstaining from Thy communion become a prey to the spiritual wolf. Therefore, I pray Thee, O Lord, Who alone art holy, sanctify my soul and body, my mind and heart, my emotions and affections, and wholly renew me. Root the fear of Thee in my members, and make Thy sanctification indelible in me. Be also my helper and defender, guide my life in peace, and make me worthy to stand on Thy right hand with Thy Saints: through the prayers and intercessions of Thy ✠ immaculate Mother, of Thy ministering Angels, of the immaculate Powers and of all the Saints who have ever been pleasing to Thee.

Amen.

PRAYER OF SAINT SYMEON THE TRANSLATOR

O only pure and sinless Lord, Who through the ineffable compassion of Thy love for men didst assume our whole nature through the pure and virgin blood of her who supernaturally conceived Thee by the coming of the Divine Spirit and by the will of the Eternal Father; O Christ Jesus, Wisdom and Peace and Power of God, Who in Thy assumption of our nature didst suffer Thy life-giving and saving Passion - the Cross, the Nails, the Spear, and Death - mortify all the deadly passions of my body.

Thou Who in Thy burial didst spoil the dominions of hell, bury with good thoughts my evil schemes and scatter the spirits of wickedness. Thou Who by Thy life-giving Resurrection on the third day didst raise up our fallen first Parent, raise me up who am sunk in sin and suggest to me ways of repentance. Thou Who by Thy glorious Ascension didst deify our nature which Thou hadst assumed and didst honor it by Thy session at the right hand of the Father, make me worthy by partaking of Thy holy Mysteries of a place at Thy right hand among those who are saved.

Thou Who by the descent of the Spirit, the Paraclete, didst make Thy holy Disciples worthy vessels, make me also a recipient of His coming. Thou Who art to come again to judge the World with justice, grant me also to meet Thee on the clouds, my Maker and Creator, with all Thy Saints, that I may unendingly glorify and praise Thee with Thy Eternal Father and Thy all-holy and good and life-giving Spirit, now and ever, and to the ages of ages. Amen.

FIRST PRAYER OF SAINT JOHN DAMASCENE

O Sovereign Lord Jesus Christ our God, Who alone hast authority to forgive men their sins, overlook in Thy goodness and love for men all my offences whether committed with knowledge or in ignorance, and make me worthy to receive without condemnation Thy divine, glorious, spotless, and life-giving Mysteries, not for punishment, nor for an increase of sins, but for purification and sanctification and as a pledge of the life and kingdom to come, as a protection and help, and for the destruction of enemies, and for the blotting out of my many transgressions. For Thou art a God of mercy and compassion and love for men, and to Thee we send up the glory, with the Father and the Holy Spirit, now and ever, and to the ages of ages. Amen.

SECOND PRAYER OF SAINT BASIL THE GREAT

I know, O Lord, that I partake of Thy immaculate Body and precious Blood unworthily, and that I am guilty, and eat and drink judgment to myself by not discerning the Body and Blood of Thee my Christ and God. But taking courage from Thy compassion I approach Thee, for Thou hast said: "He who eats My Flesh and drinks My Blood abides in Me and I in him." Therefore have compassion, O Lord, and do not make an example of me, a sinner, but deal with me according to Thy mercy; and let these Holy Things be for my healing and purification and enlightenment and protection and salvation and sanctification of body and soul, for the turning away of every phantasy and all evil practice and diabolical activity working subconsciously in my members, for confidence and love towards Thee, for reformation of life and security, for an increase of virtue and perfection, for fulfillment of the commandments, for communion with the Holy Spirit, as a provision for eternal life, and as an acceptable defense at Thy dread Tribunal, not for judgment or for condemnation.

PRAYER OF SAINT SYMEON THE NEW THEOLOGIAN

From sullied lips, from an abominable heart, from an unclean tongue, out of a polluted soul, receive my prayer, O my Christ. Reject me not, nor my words, nor my ways, nor even my shamelessness, but give me courage to say what I desire, my Christ. And even more, teach me what to do and say. I have sinned more than the harlot who, on learning where Thou wast lodging, Bought myrrh, and dared to come and anoint thy feet, my Christ, My Lord and my God. As Thou didst not repulse her when she drew near from her heart, neither, O Word, abominate me, but grant me Thy feet to clasp and kiss, and with a flood of tears as with most precious myrrh dare to anoint them.

Wash me with my tears and purify me with them, O Word. Forgive my sins and grant me pardon. Thou knowest the multitude of my evil-doings, Thou knowest also my wounds, and Thou seest my bruises. But also Thou knowest my faith, and Thou beholdest my willingness, and Thou hearest my sighs. Nothing escapes Thee, my God, my Maker, my Redeemer, not even a tear-drop, nor part of a drop. Thine eyes know what I have not achieved, and in Thy book things not yet done are written by Thee. See my depression, see how great is my trouble, and all my sins. Take from me, O God of all, that with a clean heart, trembling mind and contrite spirit I may partake of Thy pure and all-holy Mysteries by which all who eat and drink Thee with sincerity of heart are quickened and deified. For Thou, my Lord, hast said: *"Whoever eats My Flesh and drinks My Blood abides in Me and I in Him."*

Wholly true is the word of my Lord and God. For whoever partakes of Thy divine And deifying Gifts certainly is not alone, but is with Thee, my Christ, light of the Triune Sun which illumines the world. And that I may not remain alone without Thee, the Giver of Life, my Breath, my Life, my Joy, the Salvation of the world. Therefore I have drawn near to Thee as Thou seest, with tears and with a contrite spirit. Ransom of my offences, I beseech Thee to receive me, and that I may partake without condemnation of Thy life-giving and perfect Mysteries, that Thou mayest remain as Thou hast said with me, three times-wretched as I am, lest the tempter may find me without Thy grace and craftily seize me, and having deceived me, may seduce me, from Thy deifying words.

Therefore I fall at Thy feet and fervently cry to Thee: As Thou receivedst the Prodigal and the Harlot who drew near to Thee, So have compassion and receive me, the profligate and the prodigal, as with contrite spirit I now draw near to Thee. I know, O Savior, that no other has sinned against Thee as I, nor has done the deeds that I have committed. But this again I know that not the greatness of my offences nor the multitude of my sins surpasses the great patience of my God, and His extreme love for men. But with the oil of compassion those who fervently repent Thou dost purify and enlighten and makest them children of the light, sharers of Thy Divine Nature. And Thou dost act most generously,

For what is strange to Angels and to the minds of men often Thou tellest to them as to Thy true friends. These things make me bold, my Christ, these things give me wings, and I take courage from the wealth of Thy goodness to us. And rejoicing and trembling at once, I who am straw partake of fire, and, strange wonder! I am ineffably bedewed, like the bush of old which burnt without being consumed. Therefore with thankful mind, and with thankful heart, and with thankfulness in all the members of my soul and body, I worship and magnify and glorify Thee, my God, for Thou art blessed, now and throughout the ages.

SECOND PRAYER OF SAINT JOHN CHRYSOSTOM

I am not worthy, O Lord and Master, that Thou shouldest enter under the roof of my soul; but since Thou in Thy love for men dost will to dwell in me, I take courage and approach. Thou commandest: I will open wide the doors which Thou alone didst create, that Thou mayest enter with love as is Thy nature, enter and enlighten my darkened thought. I believe that Thou wilt do this, for Thou didst not banish the Harlot who approached Thee with tears, nor didst Thou reject the Publican who repented, nor didst Thou drive away the Thief who acknowledged Thy Kingdom, nor didst Thou leave the repentant persecutor (Paul) to himself; but all who had been brought to Thee by repentance Thou didst set in the company of Thy friends, O Thou Who alone art blessed always, now and to endless ages. Amen.

THIRD PRAYER OF SAINT JOHN CHRYSOSTOM

Lord Jesus Christ my God, remit, forgive, absolve and pardon the sins, offences and transgressions which I, Thy sinful, useless and unworthy servant have committed from my youth, up to the present day and hour, whether with knowledge or in ignorance, whether by words or deeds or intentions or thoughts, and whether by habit or through any of my senses. And through the intercession of her who conceived Thee without seed, the immaculate and ever-virgin Mary Thy Mother, my only sure hope and protection and salvation, make me worthy without condemnation to receive Thy pure, immortal, life-giving and dread Mysteries, for forgiveness of sins and for eternal life, for sanctification and enlightenment and strength and healing and health of soul and body, and for the blotting out and complete destruction of my evil reasonings and intentions and prejudices and nocturnal fantasies of dark evil spirits. For Thine is the kingdom and the power and the glory and the honor and the worship, with the Father and the Holy Spirit, now and ever, and to the ages of ages. Amen.

SECOND PRAYER OF SAINT JOHN DAMASCENE

I stand before the doors of Thy sanctuary, yet I do not put away my terrible thoughts. But O Christ our God, Who didst justify the Publican, and have mercy on the Canaanite woman, and didst open the gates of Paradise to the Thief, open to me the depths of Thy love for men, and as I approach and touch Thee, receive me like the Harlot and the woman with an issue of blood. For the one received healing easily by touching the hem of Thy garment, and the other by clasping Thy sacred feet obtained release from her sins. And I, in my pitiableness, dare to receive Thy whole Body. Let me not be burnt, but receive me even as these; enlighten the senses of my soul, and burn the stains of my sins: through the intercessions of her who bore Thee without seed, and of the Heavenly Powers, for Thou art blessed to the ages of ages. Amen.

FOURTH PRAYER OF SAINT JOHN CHRYSOSTOM

I believe, O Lord, and I confess that Thou art truly the Christ, the Son of the Living God, Who came into the world to save sinners, of whom I am the chief. And I believe that this is Thy pure Body and Thy own precious Blood. Therefore, I pray Thee, have mercy on me and forgive my transgressions, voluntary and involuntary, in word and deed, known and unknown. And grant that I may partake of Thy Holy Mysteries without condemnation, for the remission of sins and for life eternal. Amen.

LINES OF SAINT SYMEON THE TRANSLATOR

Behold I approach for Divine Communion. O Creator, let me not be burnt by communicating, for Thou art Fire which burns the unworthy. But purify me from every stain.

Then this Prayer:

Of Thy Mystical Supper, O Son of God, accept me today as a communicant; for I will not speak of the Mystery to Thy enemies; I will not give Thee a kiss like Judas; but like the Thief do I confess Thee. Remember me, O Lord, in Thy Kingdom.

And again these lines:

Tremble, O man, when you see the deifying Blood, for it is a coal that burns the unworthy. The Body of God both deifies and nourishes; it deifies the spirit and wondrously nourishes the mind.

And these Troparia:

Thou hast ravished me with longing, O Christ, and with Thy divine love Thou hast changed me. But burn up with spiritual fire my sins and make me worthy to be filled with delight in Thee, that I may leap for joy, O gracious Lord, and magnify Thy two comings.

Into the splendor of Thy Saints how shall I who am unworthy enter? For if I dare to enter the bridechamber, my vesture betrays me, for it is not a wedding garment, and as a prisoner I shall be cast out by the Angels. Cleanse my soul from pollution and save me, O Lord, in Thy love for men.

And this Prayer:

Sovereign Lover of men, Lord Jesus my God, let not these Holy Things be to me for judgment through my being unworthy, but for the purification and sanctification of my soul and body, and as a pledge of the life and kingdom to come. For it is good for me to cling to God and to place in the Lord my hope of salvation.

COMMON COMMUNION PRAYERS

He who eats my flesh and drinks my blood abides in me and I in him." - *John 6:56*

Prayer gives you communication with God and deepens the joy of sonship. When, prepared with prayer, you proceed to communion of the Body and Blood of Christ, then you experience the union with Him as a reality. So come to the source of deification with faith that this is why you were created: to become a partaker of the divine nature (2 Peter 1:4).

PRAYER BEFORE COMMUNION:

I believe O Lord, and I confess that Thou art truly the Christ, the Son of the Living God, who earnest into the world to save sinners, of whom I am first I believe also that this is truly Thine own pure Body, and that this is truly Thine own precious Blood. Therefore I pray Thee: have mercy upon me and for- give my transgressions both voluntary and involuntary, of word and of deed, committed in knowledge and in ignorance. And make me worthy to partake without condemnation of Thy most pure Mysteries, for the remission of my sins, and unto life everlasting. Amen.

Of Thy Mystical Supper, O Son of God, accept me today as a communicant for I will not speak of Thy Mystery to Thine enemies, neither like Judas will I give Thee a kiss; but like the thief will I confess Thee: Remember me, O Lord, in Thy Kingdom.

May the communion of Thy Holy Mysteries be neither to my judgment, nor to my condemnation, O Lord, but to the healing of soul and body.

PRAYER AFTER COMMUNION:

I thank Thee, O Lord my God, for Thou hast not rejected me, a sinner, but hast made me worthy to be a partaker of Thy Holy Things. I thank Thee, for Thou hast permitted me, the unworthy, to commune of Thy most pure and Heavenly Gifts.

But, O Master who lovest mankind, who for our sakes didst die and rise again, and gavest us these awesome and life creating Mysteries for the good and sanctification of our souls and bodies; let them be for the healing of our soul and body, the repelling of every adversary, the illumining of the eyes of my heart, the peace of my spiritual power, a faith unashamed, a love unfeigned, the fulfilling of wisdom, the observing of Thy commandments, the receiving of Thy divine grace, and the attaining of Thy Kingdom.

Preserved by them in Thy holiness, may I always remember Thy grace and live not for myself alone, but for Thee, our Master and Benefactor. May I pass from this life in the hope of eternal life, and so attain to the everlasting rest, where the voice of those who feast is unceasing, and the gladness of those who behold the goodness of Thy countenance is unending. For Thou art the true desire and the ineffable joy of those who love Thee, O Christ our God and all creation sings Thy praise forever, Amen.

THANKSGIVING AFTER HOLY COMMUNION

✛ Glory to Thee, O God; Glory to Thee. *(bow)*

✛ Glory to Thee, O God; Glory to Thee. *(bow)*

✛ Glory to Thee, O God; Glory to Thee. *(bow)*

I thank Thee, O Lord my God, that Thou hast not rejected me, a sinner, but hast granted me to be a communicant of Thy holy Things. I thank Thee that Thou hast granted me, unworthy as I am, to partake of Thy pure and heavenly Gifts. But, O Lord, Lover of men, Who didst die for us and rise again and bestow upon us these Thy dread and life-giving Mysteries for the wellbeing and sanctification of our souls and bodies, grant that these may be even to me for the healing of my soul and body, for the averting of everything hostile, for the enlightenment of the eyes of my heart, for the peace of the powers of my soul, for unashamed faith, for sincere love, for the fullness of wisdom, for the keeping of Thy commandments, for an increase of Thy divine grace, and for familiarity with Thy Kingdom; that being kept by Them in Thy holiness I may ever remember Thy grace, and never live for myself but for Thee our Lord and Benefactor. And so when I have passed from existence here in the hope of eternal life, may I attain to everlasting rest, where the song is unceasing of those who keep festival and the joy is boundless of those who behold the ineffable beauty of Thy face. For Thou art the true desire and the unutterable gladness of those who love Thee, O Christ our God, and all creation sings of Thee throughout the ages.

PRAYER OF SAINT BASIL THE GREAT

Lord Christ our God, King of the ages and Creator of all, I thank Thee for all the blessings Thou hast granted me and for the communion of Thy pure and life-giving Mysteries. I pray Thee, therefore, good Lord and Lover of men, guard me under Thy protection and within the shadow of Thy wings; and grant me with a clear conscience till my last breath worthily to partake of Thy holy Things for forgiveness of sins and for life eternal. For Thou art the Bread of Life, the Source of Holiness, the Giver of all that is good, and to Thee we send up the glory, with the Father and the Holy Spirit, now and ever, and to the ages of ages. Amen.

PRAYER OF SAINT SYMEON THE TRANSLATOR

O Thou Who givest me willingly Thy Flesh for food, Thou Who art fire, and burnest the unworthy, scorch me not, O my Maker, but rather pass through me for the integration of my members, into all my joints, my affections, and my heart. Burn up the thorns of all my sins. Purify my soul, sanctify my mind; strengthen my knees and bones; enlighten the simplicity of my five senses. Nail down the whole of me with Thy fear. Ever protect, guard, and keep me from every soul-destroying word and act. Sanctify, purify, attune, and rule me. Adorn me, give me understanding, and enlighten me. Make me the habitation of Thy Spirit alone, and no longer a habitation of sin, that as Thy house from the entry of communion every evil spirit and passion may flee from me like fire. I offer Thee as intercessors all the sanctified, the Commanders of the Bodiless Hosts, Thy Forerunner, the wise Apostles, and Thy pure and immaculate Mother. Receive their prayers, my compassionate Christ. And make Thy slave a child of light. For Thou alone art our sanctification, O Good One, and the radiance of our souls, and to Thee as our Lord and God as is right we all give glory day and night.

May Thy Holy Body, O Lord Jesus Christ our God, be to me for eternal life, and Thy Precious Blood for forgiveness of sins. And may this Eucharist be to me for joy, health, and gladness. And in Thy awful second coming, make me, a sinner, worthy to stand on the right hand of Thy glory, through the intercessions of Thy holy and most pure Mother and of all Thy Saints. Amen.

TO THE MOST HOLY MOTHER OF GOD

All-holy Lady, Mother of God, the light of my darkened soul, my hope and protection, my refuge and consolation, and my joy, I thank thee that thou hast made me, who am unworthy, worthy to be a communicant of the immaculate Body and precious Blood of thy Son. But do thou who didst bear the true Light enlighten the spiritual eyes of my heart. O thou who didst conceive the Source of Immortality, give life to me who am dead in sin. O thou who art the compassionately loving Mother of the merciful God, have mercy on me and give me compunction and contrition of heart, humility in my thoughts, and the recall of my reasoning powers from their captivity. And grant me till my last breath to receive without condemnation the sanctification of the Holy Mysteries for the healing of soul and body. And give me tears of repentance and confession, and of thanksgiving, that I may praise and glorify thee all the days of my life. For thou art blessed and glorified for ever. Amen.

SONG OF SYMEON

Now lettest Thou Thy servant depart in peace, O Lord, according to Thy word. For my eyes have seen Thy salvation which Thou hast prepared in the sight of all peoples, the light of revelation for the Gentiles, and the glory of Thy people Israel.

✛ Holy God, Holy Mighty, Holy Immortal One, have mercy on us. *(Three Times)*

✛ Glory to the Father, and to the Son, and to the Holy Spirit, now and ever, and to the ages of ages. Amen.

Most Holy ✛ Trinity, have mercy on us. O Lord, wash away our sins, O Master, pardon our transgressions. O Holy One, visit and heal our infirmities, for Thy Name's sake.
Lord, have mercy. *(Three Times)*

✛ Glory to the Father, and to the Son, and to the Holy Spirit, now and ever, and to the ages of ages. Amen.

Our Father, Who art in heaven, hallowed be Thy Name. Thy Kingdom come. Thy will be done, on earth as it is in heaven.

Give us this day our daily bread. And forgive us our debts as we forgive our debtors. And lead us not into temptation; but deliver us from the evil one.

For Thine is the kingdom, the power and the glory, of the ✝ Father, and of the Son, and of the Holy Spirit, now and ever, and to the ages of ages. Amen.

Grace like a flame shining forth from thy mouth has illumined the universe, and disclosed to the world treasures of poverty, and shown us the height of humility. And as by thy own words thou teachest us, Father John Chrysostom, so intercede with the Word, Christ our God, to save our souls.

✝ Glory to the Father, and to the Son, and to the Holy Spirit.

Thou hast received divine grace from heaven, and with thy lips dost thou teach all men to adore the one God in three Persons. O John Chrysostom, most blessed Saint, we rightly praise thee; for thou art our teacher, revealing divine things.

Now and ever, and to the ages of ages. Amen.

O Unfailing Intercessor of Christians, O Constant Mediatress before the Creator, despise not the cry of prayer of us sinners but, of thy goodness, come speedily to the help of us who in faith call upon thee. Hasten to offer swift intercession and prayer (for us), O Mother of God, whoever intercedest for those who honor thee.

Lord, have mercy. *(Twelve Times)*

✝ Glory to the Father, and to the Son, and to the Holy Spirit, now and ever, and to the ages of ages. Amen.

More honorable than the Cherubim, and incomparably more glorious than the Seraphim, thou who in virginity didst bear God the Word, thee, true Mother of God, we magnify.

SELECTED LITURGICAL HYMNS

THE PASCHAL TROPARION:

Christ is risen from the dead, trampling down death by death, and upon those in the tombs bestowing life!

HYPAKOE:

Before the dawn, Mary and the women came and found the stone rolled away from the tomb. They heard the angelic voice: "Why do you seek among the dead as a man the One who is Everlasting Light? Behold the clothes in the grave! Go and proclaim to the world: The Lord is risen!" He has slain death, as He is the Son of God, saving the race of men.

PASCHAL HYMN TO THE THEOTOKOS:

The angel cried to the Lady Full of Grace: Rejoice, O Pure Virgin! Again I say: Rejoice! Your Son is risen from His three days in the tomb! With Himself He has raised all the dead! Rejoice all ye people!

Shine! Shine! O New Jerusalem! The Glory of the Lord has shone on you! Exalt now and be glad, O Zion! Be radiant, O Pure Theotokos, in the Resurrection of your Son!

HYMN TO THE RESURRECTION:

Having beheld the Resurrection of Christ, let us worship the holy Jesus, the only Sinless One! We venerate Thy Cross, O Christ, and Thy Holy Resurrection we praise and glorify; for Thou art our God, and we know no other than Thee; we call on Thy name. Come, all you faithful, let us venerate Christ's Holy Resurrection! For, behold, through the Cross joy has come into all the world. Ever blessing the Lord, let us praise His Resurrection. By enduring the Cross for us, He destroyed death by death!

TROPARION OF ASCENSION:

O Christ God, Thou hast ascended in glory, granting joy to Thy disciples by the promise of the Holy Spirit. Through the blessing they were assured that Thou art the Son of God, the Redeemer of the world!

TROPARION OF PENTECOST:

Blessed art Thou, O Christ our God, who hast revealed the fishermen as most wise by sending down upon them the Holy Spirit; through them Thou didst draw the world into Thy net. O Lover of Man, glory to Thee!

TROPARION OF THE CROSS:

O Lord, save Thy people, and bless Thine inheritance. Grant victories to the Orthodox Christians over their adversaries; and by the virtue of Thy Cross, preserve Thy habitation.

TROPARION OF THE NATIVITY:

Thy Nativity, O Christ our God, has shone to the world the light of wisdom! For by it those who worshipped the stars were taught by a star to adore Thee, the Sun of Righteousness, and to know Thee, the Orient from on high! O Lord, glory to Thee!

TROPARION OF THE EPIPHANY:

When Thou, O Lord, wast baptized in the Jordan, the worship of the Trinity was made manifest! For the voice of the Father bare witness to Thee, and called Thee His beloved Son! And the Spirit, in the form of a dove, confirmed the truthfulness of His word. O Christ our God, who hast revealed Thyself, and hast enlightened the world, glory to Thee!

TROPARION OF THE ANNUNCIATION:

Today is the beginning of our salvation, the revelation of the eternal mystery! The Son of God becomes the Son of the

Virgin, as Gabriel announces the coming of Grace. Together with him let us cry to the ✚ Theotokos: Rejoice, O Full of Grace! The Lord is with you!

TROPARION OF THE TRANSFIGURATION:

Thou wast transfigured on the mount, O Christ God, revealing Thy glory to the disciples as far as they could bear it. Let Thine everlasting light shine upon us sinners! Through the prayers of the ✚ Theotokos, O Giver of Light, glory to Thee!

LENTEN PRAYER OF EPHRAIM THE SYRIAN:

O Lord and Master of my life, take from me the spirit of sloth, despair, lust of power, and idle talk. But give rather the spirit of chastity, humility, patience, and love to Thy servant. Yea, O Lord and King, grant me to see my own sins, and not to judge my brother, for Thou art blessed unto ages of ages. Amen.

Then, 13 Bows, saying the Jesus Prayer, or these prayers:

Lord Jesus Christ, Son of God, have mercy on me, a sinner. *(Bow)*

God be merciful to me a sinner. *(Bow)*

God, cleanse me of my sins and have mercy on me. *(Bow)*

Thou hast created me; Lord, have mercy on me. *(Bow)*

I have sinned immeasurably; Lord, forgive me. *(Bow)*

Lord Jesus Christ. Son of God, have mercy on me, a sinner. *(Bow)*

God be merciful to me a sinner. *(Bow)*

God, cleanse me of my sins and have mercy on me. *(Bow)*

Thou hast created me; Lord, have mercy on me. *(Bow)*

I have sinned immeasurably; Lord, forgive me. *(Bow)*

God be merciful to me a sinner. *(Bow)*
Thou hast created me; Lord, have mercy on me. *(Bow)*

I have sinned immeasurably; Lord, forgive me. *(Bow)*

Then Repeat the Prayer of Saint Ephraim the Syrian:

O Lord and Master of my life, take from me the spirit of sloth, despair, lust of power, and idle talk. But give rather the spirit of chastity, humility, patience, and love to Thy servant. Yea, O Lord and King, grant me to see my own sins, and not to judge my brother, for Thou art blessed unto ages of ages. Amen.

(The following four Prayers are from the book, "Domestic Rule")

THE FIRST PRAYER OF SAINT ISAAC THE SYRIAN

O Lord Jesus Christ my God, Who dost visit Thy creation, to Thee are manifest my passions, and the frailty of my nature, and the strength of my adversary.

Do Thou Thyself, O Master, protect me from his malice, because his power is strong, whereas my nature is passionate and my strength is feeble.

Do Thou, O Good One, Who knowest my weakness and hast borne the difficulties of my impotence, guard me against disordered thoughts and the flood of passions, and make me worthy of this holy service, lest in my passions I spoil its sweetness and be found impudent and audacious in Thy sight.

But in Thy mercy have mercy on me: For blessed art Thou unto the ages. Amen.

THE SECOND PRAYER OF SAINT STEPHEN OF THE THEBAID

O Master and Lord, Jesus Christ my God, be Thou my helper. I am in Thy hands. Suffer me not to sin for I am tempted; suffer me not to perish in my sins.
Take pity upon Thy creature. Cast me not away from Thy face on account of my sins, for to Thee have I fled.

Heal my soul, for I have sinned against Thee. Before Thee are all they that afflict me and seek after my soul to destroy it: I have no other refuge than in Thee, O Lord; save me for the sake of Thy mercy, O Lord, for Thou art powerful in all things, O Lord.

For Thine is the kingdom and the power and the glory, with the Father and the Holy Spirit, now and ever, and unto the ages of ages. Amen.

THE THIRD PRAYER OF SAINT JOHN CHRYSOSTOM

O Lord, whether I will it or not, save me. As a filthy lover of material things I desire sinful defilement, but as Thou art good and all-powerful, Thou canst hold me back.

For if Thou hast mercy on a righteous man, it is no great thing; if Thou savest a pure man, it is nothing wonderful, since they are deserving of Thy mercy.

Rather, make known the wonder of Thy mercy in me, who am wretched, sinful and defiled, and show Thy compassion.

Poor in all good works, I am a pauper, abandoned to Thee.

O Lord, save me for Thy mercy's sake: For blessed art Thou unto the ages. Amen.

THE FOURTH PRAYER

Master, have mercy on me for the sake of Thy goodness, and suffer me not to go astray from Thy will.

And cast not my poor prayers away from Thy face, but hear, O Lord, the voice of my prayer when I pray to Thee in the day and in the night, and accept it as choice incense.

Withhold not Thy grace on account of my sins, but save me for Thy holy Name's sake.

For Thine alone it is to show mercy and save us, and unto Thee do we send up glory, to the ✠ Father and to the Son, and to the Holy Spirit, now and ever, and unto the ages of ages. Amen.

Then, having purified yourself by prayer; kiss the cross which you wear upon your breast, and make the Sign of the Cross with it, and say:

✠ Lord Jesus Christ, Son of God, bless, sanctify and protect me by the power of Thy life-giving Cross.

AKATHIST TO OUR MOST HOLY LADY, MOTHER OF GOD

KONTAKION I

Queen of the Heavenly Host, Defender of our souls, we thy servants offer to thee songs of victory and thanksgiving, for thou, O Mother of God, hast delivered us from dangers. But as thou hast invincible power, free us from conflicts of all kinds that we may cry to thee: Rejoice, unwedded Bride!

OIKOS I

An Archangel was sent from Heaven to say to the Mother of God: Rejoice! And seeing Thee, O Lord, taking bodily form, he was amazed and with his bodiless voice he stood crying to her such things as these:

Rejoice, thou through whom joy will flash forth!

Rejoice, thou through whom the curse will cease!

Rejoice, revival of fallen Adam!

Rejoice, redemption of the tears of Eve!

Rejoice, height hard to climb for human thoughts!

Rejoice, depth hard to contemplate even for the eyes of Angels!

Rejoice, thou who art the King's throne!

Rejoice, thou who bearest Him Who bears all!

Rejoice, star that casuist the Sun to appear!

Rejoice, womb of the divine incarnation!

Rejoice, thou through whom creation becomes new!

Rejoice, thou through whom the Creator becomes a babe!

Rejoice, unwedded Bride!

KONTAKION II

Aware that she was living in chastity, the holy Virgin said boldly to Gabriel: "Thy strange message is hard for my soul to accept. How is it thou speakest of the birth from a seedless conception?" And she cried: Alleluia!

OIKOS II

Seeking to know what passes knowledge, the Virgin cried to the ministering spirit: "Tell me, how can a son be born from a chaste womb?" Then he spoke to her in fear, only crying aloud thus:

Rejoice, initiate of God's ineffable will!

Rejoice, assurance of those who pray in silence!

Rejoice, prelude of Christ's miracles!

Rejoice, crown of His dogmas!

Rejoice, heavenly ladder by which God came down!

Rejoice, bridge that conveys us from earth to heaven!

Rejoice, wonder of angels blazed abroad!

Rejoice, wound of demons bewailed afar!

Rejoice, thou who ineffably gavest birth to the Light!

Rejoice, thou who didst reveal thy secret to none!

Rejoice, thou who surpasses! the knowledge of the wise!

Rejoice, thou who gives light to the minds of the faithful!

Rejoice, unwedded Bride!

KONTAKION III

The power of the Most High then overshadowed the Virgin for conception, and showed her fruitful womb as a sweet meadow to all who wish to reap salvation, as they sing: Alleluia!

OIKOS III

Pregnant with the Divine indwelling the Virgin ran to Elizabeth whose unborn babe at once recognized her embrace, rejoiced, and with leaps of joy as songs, cried to the Mother of God:

Rejoice, scion of an undying Shoot!

Rejoice, field of untainted fruit!

Rejoice, thou who laborest for Him Whose labor is love!

Rejoice, thou who gives birth to the Father of our life!

Rejoice, corn land yielding a rich crop of mercies!

Rejoice, table bearing a wealth of forgiveness!

Rejoice, thou who revives the garden of delight!

Rejoice, thou who preparest a haven for souls!

Rejoice, acceptable incense of intercession!

Rejoice, purification of all the world!

Rejoice, favor of God to mortals!

Rejoice, access of mortals to God!

Rejoice, unwedded Bride!

KONTAKION IV

Sustaining from within a storm of doubtful thoughts, the chaste Joseph was troubled. For knowing thee to have no husband, he suspected a secret union, O Immaculate One. But when he learned that thy conception was of the Holy Spirit, he exclaimed: Alleluia!

OIKOS IV

The shepherds heard Angels caroling Christ's incarnate Presence, and running like sheep to their shepherd, they beheld him as an innocent Lamb fed at Mary's breast, and they sang to her and said:

Rejoice, mother of the Lamb and the Shepherd!

Rejoice, fold of spiritual sheep!

Rejoice, defense against invisible enemies!

Rejoice, key to the gates of Paradise!

Rejoice, for the things of Heaven rejoice with the earth!

Rejoice, for the things of earth join chorus with the Heavens!

Rejoice, never-silent voice of the Apostles!

Rejoice, invincible courage of the martyrs!

Rejoice, firm support of faith!

Rejoice, radiant blaze of grace!

Rejoice, thou through whom hell was stripped bare!

Rejoice, thou through whom we are clothed with glory!

Rejoice, unwedded Bride!

KONTAKION V

Having sighted the divinely moving star, the Wise Men followed its light and held it as a lamp by which they sought a powerful King. And as they approached the Unapproachable, they rejoiced and shouted to Him: Alleluia!

OIKOS V

The sons of the Chaldees saw in the hands of the Virgin Him Who with His hand 'made man. And knowing Him to be the Lord although He had taken the form of a servant, they hastened to worship Him with their gifts and cried to her who is blessed:

Rejoice, mother of the never-setting Star!

Rejoice, dawn of the mystic Day! Rejoice, thou who didst enlighten the initiates of the Trinity!

Rejoice, thou who didst banish from power the inhuman tyrant!

Rejoice, thou who hast shown us Christ as the Lord and Lover of men!

Rejoice, thou who redeemest from pagan worship!

Rejoice, thou who dost drag from the mire of works!

Rejoice, thou who hast stopped the worship of fire!

Rejoice, thou who hast quenched the flame of the passions!

Rejoice, guide of the faithful to chastity!

Rejoice, joy of all generations!

Rejoice, unwedded Bride!

KONTAKION VI

Turned God-bearing heralds, the Wise Men returned to Babylon. They fulfilled Thy prophecy and to all preached Thee as the Christ, and they left Herod as a trifler, who could not sing: Alleluia!

OIKOS VI

By shining in Egypt the light of truth, Thou didst dispel the darkness of falsehood, O Savior. For, unable to endure Thy strength, its idols fell; and those who were freed from their spell cried to the Mother of God:

Rejoice, uplifting of men!

Rejoice, downfall of demons!

Rejoice, thou who hast trampled on the delusion of error!

Rejoice, thou who hast exposed the fraud of idols!

Rejoice, sea that has drowned the spiritual Pharaoh!

Rejoice, rock that has refreshed those thirsting for Life!

Rejoice, pillar of fire guiding those in darkness!

Rejoice, shelter of the world broader than a cloud!

Rejoice, sustenance replacing Manna!

Rejoice, minister of holy delight!

Rejoice, land of promise!

Rejoice, thou from whom flows milk and honey!

Rejoice, unwedded Bride!

KONTAKION VII

When Simeon was about to depart this life of delusion, Thou wast brought as a Babe to him. But he recognized Thee as also perfect God, and marveling at Thy ineffable wisdom, he cried: Alleluia!

OIKOS VII

The Creator showed us a new creation when He appeared to us who came from Him. For He sprang from an unsown womb and kept it chaste as it was, that seeing the miracle we might sing to her and say:

Rejoice, flower of incorruption!

Rejoice, crown of continence!

Rejoice, flashing symbol of the resurrection!

Rejoice, mirror of the life of the Angels!

Rejoice, tree of glorious fruit by which the faithful are nourished!

Rejoice, bush of shady leaves by which many are sheltered!

Rejoice, thou who. bearest the Guide of those astray!

Rejoice, thou who gives birth to the Redeemer of captives!

Rejoice, pleader before the Just Judge!

Rejoice, forgiveness of many sinners!

Rejoice, robe of freedom for the naked!

Rejoice, love that vanquishes all desire!

Rejoice, unwedded Bride!

KONTAKION VIII

Seeing the Child Exile, let us be exiles from the world and transport our minds to Heaven. For the Most High God appeared on earth as lowly man, because He wished to draw to the heights those who cry to Him: Alleluia!

OIKOS VIII

Wholly present was the infinite Word among those here below, yet in no way absent from those on high; for this was a divine condescension and not a change of place. And His birth was from a God-possessed Virgin who heard words like these:

Rejoice, container of the uncontainable God!

Rejoice, door of solemn mystery!

Rejoice, doubtful report of unbelievers!

Rejoice, undoubted boast of the faithful!

Rejoice, all-holy chariot of Him Who rides on the Cherubim!

Rejoice, all-glorious temple of Him Who is above the Seraphim!

Rejoice, thou who hast united opposites!

Rejoice, thou who hast joined virginity and motherhood!

Rejoice, thou through Whom sin has been absolved!

Rejoice, thou through whom Paradise is opened!

Rejoice, key to the Kingdom of Christ!

Rejoice, hope of eternal blessings!

Rejoice, unwedded Bride!

KONTAKION IX

All angel kind was amazed at the great act of Thy incarnation; for they saw the inaccessible God as a man accessible to all, dwelling with us and hearing from all: Alleluia!

OIKOS IX

We see most eloquent orators dumb as fish before Thee, O Mother of God. For they dare not ask: How canst Thou bear a Child and yet remain a Virgin? But we marvel at the mystery, and cry with faith:

Rejoice, receptacle of the Wisdom of God!

Rejoice, treasury of His Providence!

Rejoice, thou who showiest philosophers to be fools!

Rejoice, thou who constraints the learned to silence!

Rejoice, for the clever critics have made fools of themselves!

Rejoice, for the writers of myths have died out!

Rejoice, thou who didst break the webs of the Athenians!

Rejoice, thou who didst fill the nets of the fishermen!

Rejoice, thou who drawest us from the depths of ignorance!

Rejoice, thou who enlightens many with knowledge!

Rejoice, ship of those who wish to be saved!

Rejoice, haven for sailors on the sea of life!

Rejoice, unwedded Bride!

KONTAKION X

Wishing to save the world, the Ruler of all came to it spontaneously. And though as God He is our Shepherd, for us He appeared to us as a Man; and having called mankind to salvation by His own Perfect Manhood, as God He hears: Alleluia!

OIKOS X

Thou art a wall to virgins and to all who run to thee, O Virgin Mother of God. For the Maker of heaven and earth prepared thee, O Immaculate One, and dwelt in thy womb, and taught all to call to thee:

Rejoice, pillar of virginity!

Rejoice, gate of salvation!

Rejoice, founder of spiritual reformation!

Rejoice, leader of divine goodness!

Rejoice, for thou didst regenerate those conceived in shame!

Rejoice, for thou gavest understanding to those robbed of their senses!

Rejoice, thou who didst foil the corrupter of minds!

Rejoice, thou who gavest birth to the Sower of chastity!

Rejoice, bride chamber of a virgin marriage!

Rejoice, thou who doth wed the faithful to the Lord!

Rejoice, fair mother and nurse of virgins!

Rejoice, betrothed of holy souls!

Rejoice, unwedded Bride!

KONTAKION XI

Every hymn falls short that aspires to embrace the multitude of Thy many mercies. For if we should offer to Thee, O Holy King, songs numberless as the sand, we should still have done nothing worthy of what Thou hast given to us who shout to Thee: Alleluia!

OIKOS XI

We see the Holy Virgin as a flaming torch appearing to those in darkness. For having kindled the Immaterial Light, she leads all to divine knowledge; she illumines our minds with radiance and is honored by our shouting these praises:

Rejoice, ray of the spiritual Sun!

Rejoice, flash of unfading splendor!

Rejoice, lightning that lights up our souls!

Rejoice, thunder that stuns our enemies!

Rejoice, for thou didst cause the refulgent Light to dawn!

Rejoice, for thou didst cause the river of many-streams to gush forth!

Rejoice, living image of the font!

Rejoice, remover of the stain of sin!

Rejoice, laver that washes the conscience clean!

Rejoice, bowl for mixing the wine of joy!

Rejoice, aroma of the fragrance of Christ!

Rejoice, life of mystical festivity!

Rejoice, unwedded Bride!

KONTAKION XII

When He Who forgives all men their past debts wished to restore us to favor, of His own will He came to dwell among those who had fallen from His grace; and having torn up the record of their sins, He hears from all: Alleluia!

OIKOS XII

While singing to thy Child, we all praise thee as a living temple, O Mother of God. For the Lord Who holds all things in His hand dwelt in thy womb, and He sanctified and glorified thee, and taught all to cry to thee:

Rejoice, tabernacle of God the Word!

Rejoice, saint greater than the saints!

Rejoice, ark made golden by the Spirit!

Rejoice, inexhaustible treasury of Life!

Rejoice, precious diadem of pious kings!

Rejoice, adorable boast of devoted priests!

Rejoice, unshaken tower of the Church!

Rejoice, impregnable wall of the Kingdom!

Rejoice, thou through whom we obtain our victories!

Rejoice, thou before whom our foes fall prostrate!

Rejoice, healing of my body!

Rejoice, salvation of my soul!

Rejoice, unwedded Bride!

KONTAKION XIII

O all-praised Mother who didst bear the Word holiest of all
the Saints, accept this our offering, and deliver us from all
offense, and redeem from future torment those who cry in
unison to thee: Alleluia. *(Three Times)*

And again Oikos I and Kontakion I are read.

OIKOS I

An Archangel was sent from Heaven to say to the Mother of
God: Rejoice! And seeing Thee, O Lord, taking bodily form,
he was amazed and with his bodiless voice he stood crying to
her such things as these:

Rejoice, thou through whom joy will flash forth!

Rejoice, thou through whom the curse will cease!

Rejoice, revival of fallen Adam!

Rejoice, redemption of the tears of Eve!

Rejoice, height hard to climb for human thoughts!

Rejoice, depth hard to contemplate even for the eyes of
Angels!

Rejoice, thou who art the King's throne!

Rejoice, thou who bearest Him Who bears all!

Rejoice, star that casuist the Sun to appear!

Rejoice, womb of the divine incarnation!

Rejoice, thou through whom creation becomes new!

Rejoice, thou through whom the Creator becomes a babe!

Rejoice, unwedded Bride!

KONTAKION I

Queen of the Heavenly Host, Defender of our souls, we thy servants offer to thee songs of victory and thanksgiving, for thou, O Mother of God, hast delivered us from dangers.

But as thou hast invincible power, free us from conflicts of all kinds that we may cry to thee: Rejoice, unwedded Bride!

PRAYER TO OUR MOST HOLY LADY, MOTHER OF GOD

My most gracious Queen, my hope, Mother of God, shelter of orphans, and intercessor of travelers, strangers and pilgrims, joy of those in sorrow, protectress of the wronged, see my distress, see my affliction!

Help me, for I am helpless. Feed me, for I am a stranger and pilgrim.

Thou knowest my offense; forgive and resolve it as thou wilt. For I know no other help but thee, no other intercessor, no gracious consoler but thee, O Mother of God, to guard and protect me throughout the ages. Amen.

AKATHIST TO GREAT MARTYR-HEALER PANTELEIMON

KONTAKION 1

Chosen passion-bearer of Christ and gracious healer, who freely grantest healing to the sick, we praise thee in songs as our protector. As thou hast boldness with the Lord, free us from all harm and sickness who cry with love to thee:

Rejoice, Great Martyr and Healer Panteleimon!

Most Holy Saint and Martyr Panteleimon-the-Healer, intercede to the Most Merciful God for *(NAME)* for the healing of his/her soul and body.

OIKOS 1

We know thee, glorious Panteleimon, as an earthly angel and a heavenly man. For adorned with angelic purity and martyrdom thou hast passed from earth to Heaven, whise with angels and all the saints standing before the throne of the Lord of Glory, thou prayest for all of us on earth who venerate thee with these invocations:

Rejoice, torch of piety!

Rejoice, most glorious lamp of the Church!

Rejoice, adornment of venerable martyrs!

Rejoice, support of the faithful in unflinching endurance!

Rejoice, outstanding boast of youth!

Rejoice, warrior of Christ of invincible courage!

Rejoice, thou who having grown up in the world wast not of the world!

Rejoice, angel in the flesh, surpassing mortals!

Rejoice, all-blessed dweller in Heaven!

Rejoice, vessel of divine knowledge!

Rejoice, thou by whom faith has been exalted!

Rejoice, thou by whom delusion has been dethroned!

Rejoice, Great Martyr and Healer Panteleimon!

KONTAKION 2

Seeing thee to be a chosen vessel, the Lord loved the beauty of thy soul; for, despising all earthly glory and pleasure, thou didst long to adorn thyself with the crown of martyrdom, wounded with divine love and singing inspiringly: Alleluia!

Most Holy Saint and Martyr Panteleimon-the-Healer, intercede to the Most Merciful God for *(NAME)* for the healing of his/her soul and body.

OIKOS 2

Possessing divinely inspired knowledge, O valiant warrior Panteleimon, thou didst astound the Emperor Maximian by the courage of thy soul and by the words with which thou didst fearlessly preach Christ. Wherefore, praising thy boldness we say to thee:

Rejoice, thou who didst despise Maximian's threats!

Rejoice, thou who didst not yield to the advice of the godless!

Rejoice, propagator of true adoration!

Rejoice, uprooter of demon worship!

Rejoice, accuser of the fury of the torturers!

Rejoice, overthrower of the delusion of idols!

Rejoice, thou who didst disperse the assembly of the godless!

Rejoice, thou who didst exchange corruptible for heavenly joy!

Rejoice, converser with immaterial angels!

Rejoice, fellow-chorister of longsuffering saints!

Rejoice, thou by whom Satan was put to shame!

Rejoice, thou by whom Christ is glorified!

Rejoice, Great Martyr and Healer Panteleimon!

KONTAKION 3

By the power of the Most High given to thee and by thy strong patience thou didst render powerless the torturers insolence, O valiant victor, undaunted by fire, wild beasts, and the wheel. When beheaded with the sword, thou didst receive the crown of victory from Christ the Lord, crying to Him: Alleluia!

Most Holy Saint and Martyr Panteleimon-the-Healer, intercede to the Most Merciful God for *(NAME)* for the healing of his/her soul and body.

OIKOS 3

The monastery which hath thy precious head as a great treasure, O divinely wise martyr, is filled with joy over it, and praising with love the Grace of healing given thee by God, thankfully crieth to thee:

Rejoice, all radiant lamp of Nicomedia!

Rejoice, unsleeping guardian of the monastery that honoreth thee!

Rejoice, thou through whom godlessness grew cold!

Rejoice, thou through whom the knowledge of God hath increased!

Rejoice, bright glory of passion-bearers!

Rejoice, joyous report of the Orthodox!

Rejoice, gracious source of healings!

Rejoice, container of great gifts!

Rejoice, fragrant myrrh that doth sweeten souls!

Rejoice, for thou dost help those who call upon thee!

Rejoice, thou who didst give sight to the blind!

Rejoice, thou who didst cause the lame to walk!

Rejoice, Great Martyr and Healer Panteleimon!

KONTAKION 4

Possessed by a storm of polytheistic thoughts, the impious Emperor was confused on learning from the doctors who were jealous of thee that thou healest all kinds of incurable illnesses by the name of Christ. And we, glorifying with gladness our wonderful God in thee, cry to Him: Alleluia!

Most Holy Saint and Martyr Panteleimon-the-Healer, intercede to the Most Merciful God for (NAME) for the healing of his/her soul and body.

OIKOS 4

When the people of Nicomedia heard of thy great compassion for the suffering and of thy free healing of all illnesses, all rushed to thee with faith in the healing Grace in thee, and receiving swift healing of all their diseases they glorified God and magnified thee, their most gracious healer, crying to thee:

Rejoice, thou who art anointed with the myrrh of Grace!

Rejoice, sanctified temple of God!

Rejoice, great glory of the pious!

Rejoice, firm wall of the oppressed!

Rejoice, thou who surpassest the wise in knowledge!

Rejoice, thou who enlightenest the thoughts of the faithful!

Rejoice, recipient of divine gifts and source of many of the Lords mercies to us!

Rejoice, speedy helper of the suffering!

Rejoice, harbor of the storm-tossed!

Rejoice, instructor for those astray!

Rejoice, thou who dost heal the sick freely!

Rejoice, thou who dost impart healing abundantly!

Rejoice, Great Martyr and Healer Panteleimon!

KONTAKION 5

The Lord worked a glorious miracle through thee when, through His servant Hismolaus, He called thee into His marvelous light. For after thy prayer to Christ a child who had died from snakebite at once revived and stood up healed. Then recognizing the Life giver as the true God of all, with firm faith thou didst cry to Him: Alleluia!

Most Holy Saint and Martyr Panteleimon-the-Healer, intercede to the Most Merciful God for (NAME) for the healing of his/her soul and body.

The blind man whom thou didst touch with prayer in the name of Christ recovered his sight, O glorious Martyr. Then, renouncing thy Fathers polytheism, thou wast baptized by the priest Hermolaus and didst embrace thy mothers religion with which thou didst also enlighten thy Father. Therefore we cry aloud to thee as to a glorious servant of God and wonderful healer:

Rejoice, thou who hast great devotion to God!

Rejoice, thou who art ever aflame with the fire of divine love!

Rejoice, attentive listener to the teachings of the priest Hermolaus!

Rejoice, thou who didst follow the advice of thy mother Eubule!

Rejoice, thou who didst give away everything to obtain Christ!

Rejoice, thou who didst vanquish love for the world by love for God!

Rejoice, for instead of the pleasures of the world thou didst accept for Christ cruel sufferings!

Rejoice, for thou didst become a partner of Christ's Passion!

Rejoice, thou who didst overcome all the passions!

Rejoice, thou who through Grace wast adorned with dispassion!

Rejoice, thou who dost fill with joy those who hasten to thee!

Rejoice, thou who dost heal all freely by the Grace of Christ!

Rejoice, Great Martyr and Healer Panteleimon!

KONTAKION 6

The blind man enlightened by thee in body and soul became a preacher of the truth for, like the blind man of the Gospel, he boldly preached Christ to all as the true light that enlighteneth every man. But for reproaching the impious Emperor and the pagan gods he was beheaded and rose to the unwaning light in Heaven to sing to God: Alleluia!

Most Holy Saint and Martyr Panteleimon-the-Healer, intercede to the Most Merciful God for *(NAME)* for the healing of his/her soul and body.

OIKOS 6

Standing before the Emperors tribunal with a radiant face thou didst boldly declare in the hearing of all, thrice blessed martyr: Mine all-healing power and glory is Christ, the true God, the Lord of all, Who raiseth the dead and healeth all infirmities. For this confession we bless thee and say:

Rejoice, thundering mouth of the deity of Christ!

Rejoice, mellifluous tongue that declareth His plan of salvation!

Rejoice, orator of sublime theology!

Rejoice, wise sower of piety!

Rejoice, sweet-sounding flute of faith!

Rejoice, glorious preacher of Orthodoxy!

Rejoice, thou who wast shown to be marvelous before thy death!

Rejoice, worker of wonders after thy death!

Rejoice, seer of Christ's glory!

Rejoice, listener of those who pray to thee!

Rejoice, giver of help to those who need it!

Rejoice, obtainer of blessings for those who honor thy memory!

Rejoice, Great Martyr and Healer Panteleimon!

KONTAKION 7

Myrrh was poured out on thy soul, O divinely wise healer, from the Comforter Spirit, wherefore after thy death thy venerable relics, by their fragrance banish the stench of passions and give healing to those who with faith cry to God: Alleluia!

Most Holy Saint and Martyr Panteleimon-the-Healer, intercede to the Most Merciful God for *(NAME)* for the healing of his/her soul and body.

OIKOS 7

When the worshippers of idols beheld, O Saint, the paralyzed man raised and walking through thy prayer many believed in Christ; but the demon's priest, consumed with jealousy, incited the Emperor to anger. Therefore, to thee who was mercilessly tortured and burnt for Christ, we cry with compunction:

Rejoice, thou who didst despise earthly pleasures!

Rejoice, thou who wast above material comforts!

Rejoice, for thou didst regard as nothing all the beautiful things in this world!

Rejoice, for thou didst shake thyself free of fleeting glory!

Rejoice, thou who didst remain free from the nets of the devil!

Rejoice, thou who didst vanquish the wiles of the torturers!

Rejoice, thou who didst not spare thy life for Christ!

Rejoice, thou who wast shown to be an enemy of hostile flesh!

Rejoice, thou who didst oppress the spread of polytheism!

Rejoice, thou who by the power of God didst defeat the idols!

Rejoice, sharp arrow by which enemies are wounded!

Rejoice, mediator who defendest the faithful!

Rejoice, Great Martyr and Healer Panteleimon!

KONTAKION 8

The Lord appeared to thee in a wonderful way, encouraging and upholding thee in the tortures for His name. For in the person of the priest Hermolaus He cooled the boiling lead into which thou wast thrown, and in the sea He untied the great stone from thy neck and brought thee unharmed to land. But thou, having been brought again before the Emperor, didst sing triumphantly to Christ our God: Alleluia!

Most Holy Saint and Martyr Panteleimon-the-Healer, intercede to the Most Merciful God for *(NAME)* for the healing of his/her soul and body.

OIKOS 8

While dwelling noetically wholly in Heaven, thou leavest not those below on earth but remainest with us through the relics of thy holy skull, O great passion-bearer of Christ, receiving from the Lord enlightenment and sanctification and giving it to those who cry to thee thus:

Rejoice, thou who art filled with divine wisdom!

Rejoice, discerner of Gods providence!

Rejoice, delight of minds made wise by God!

Rejoice, gladness of souls who love God!

Rejoice, bright pearl of Christ!

Rejoice, thou who was sanctified in soul and body!

Rejoice, dweller in the courts of the firstborn in Heaven!

Rejoice, inhabitant of the ever-blessed bridal halls!

Rejoice, beholder of the light of the Trinity!

Rejoice, fervent mediator in thy prayers to God for us!

Rejoice, thou who grantest illumination to souls!

Rejoice, thou who sendest comfort to the afflicted!

Rejoice, Great Martyr and Healer Panteleimon!

KONTAKION 9

All nature marveled, O Panteleimon, at the radiance of Grace and wealth of virtues in thee: thine angelic purity, thy great courage in cruel sufferings, thy strong love for Christ and great compassion for people, for whom thou doest glorious things that they may sing: Alleluia!

Most Holy Saint and Martyr Panteleimon-the-Healer, intercede to the Most Merciful God for (NAME) for the healing of his/her soul and body.

OIKOS 9

Eloquent orators cannot worthily praise thy struggles, O glorious victor, as by the invincible power of God, though young in years thou didst conquer the ancient, primordial enemy and didst put to shame the delusion of idols. But we, filled with wonder, cry to thee:

Rejoice, joyful sight of angels!

Rejoice, reverent wonder of men!

Rejoice, thou who didst shed thy blood for Christ, and in death didst shed milk!

Rejoice, thou who didst give up thy body to a martyrs death for His sake!

Rejoice, model of confession!

Rejoice, valiant warrior of the King of kings!

Rejoice, thou who didst conquer the ruler of darkness!

Rejoice, thou who by thy victory didst gladden Heaven and earth!

Rejoice, blessed inhabitant of the world above!

Rejoice, wise pilgrim of the world below!

Rejoice, tree adorned with the fruits of the gifts of Grace!

Rejoice, thou who carriest palms of victory!

Rejoice, Great Martyr and Healer Panteleimon!

KONTAKION 10

Filled with compassion, as a true imitator of the Lord, the Giver of mercy, O venerable martyr, thou wast renamed by Him Panteleimon (that is, all-merciful), for thou pourest mercy on all who resort to thee; pour it also abundantly on us who cry to God concerning thee: Alleluia!

Most Holy Saint and Martyr Panteleimon-the-Healer, intercede to the Most Merciful God for *(NAME)* for the healing of his/her soul and body.

OIKOS 10

Finding thee a strong wall impregnable to all kinds of torture, the torturer tried to crush thy strength by the teeth of wild beast and the spikes of the torture-wheel, but all to no effect. For the power of Christ subdued the fierceness of the beasts and the frightful wheel, on which thy body was turned, immediately broke to pieces. So to thee, invincible passionbearer, we cry:

Rejoice, precious chosen one of Christ!

Rejoice, unblemished fragrance of God!

Rejoice, firm diamond of the Church!

Rejoice, unshakable tower reaching to Heaven!

Rejoice, tamer of visible beasts!

Rejoice, crusher of invisible dragons!

Rejoice, thou was wast stained with thy blood shed for Christ, mixed with milk!

Rejoice, thou who hast received unfading crowns!

Rejoice, thou who causest joy to angels and men!

Rejoice, thou who hast been glorified by God in Heaven and on earth!

Rejoice, celestial one, who singest in choir with the martyrs!

Rejoice, thou who art satisfied with the sweet vision of Christ!

Rejoice, Great Martyr and Healer Panteleimon!

KONTAKION 11

A funeral song we offer to thy sacred immolation for Christ, in which milk instead of blood flowed from thee, Great Martyr, and the olive tree under which thou wast beheaded was all covered with healing fruit. Wherefore we cry fervently to Christ Who wonderfully glorifieth those who glorify Him: Alleluia!

Most Holy Saint and Martyr Panteleimon-the-Healer, intercede to the Most Merciful God for *(NAME)* for the healing of his/her soul and body.

OIKOS 11

A luminous ray wast thou, O divinely wise one, to those sitting in the darkness of polytheism, leading them to the Sun or righteousness, Christ God. Him do thou entreat that we who offer thee these glad praises may ever live in the light of His commandments:

Rejoice, bright star, shining in the noetical firmament!

Rejoice, ray of light shining for Christian people!

Rejoice, thou wast mystically illumined by the Sun, Christ!

Rejoice, thou who in spirit roamest the earth!

Rejoice, beautiful tabernacle of the Most Holy Spirit!

Rejoice, honorable vessel that poureth out healing!

Rejoice, treasury of purity!

Rejoice, namesake of mercy!

Rejoice, heir of the Heavenly Kingdom!

Rejoice, partaker of eternal glory!

Rejoice, patron of those in distress on the sea of life!

Rejoice, unmercenary healer who helpest those who invoke thee with faith!

Rejoice, Great Martyr and Healer Panteleimon!

KONTAKION 12

Thou didst receive an abundance of Grace, thrice-blessed one, according to the greatness of thy love for Christ God, Who also showed thee to be a source of healing, for thou curest free of charge the sicknesses of soul and body of those who come to thee with faith and cry to God: Alleluia!

Most Holy Saint and Martyr Panteleimon-the-Healer, intercede to the Most Merciful God for *(NAME)* for the healing of his/her soul and body.

OIKOS 12

Chanting of thy long-suffering labors for Christ, O glorious passion-bearer, we praise thy great patience, we bless thy martyrs death, and we honor thy holy memory, O our defender and healer, and in praise we cry to thee:

Rejoice, sweet-sounding trumpet of piety!

Rejoice, sword which cuts down impiety!

Rejoice, thou who wast scraped on a tree for Him Who stretched out His arms on the tree of the Cross!

Rejoice, for, being burnt for Him, thou didst extinguish the furnace of delusion!

Rejoice, thou who didst wound the enemies by thy wounds!

Rejoice, thou who didst dry the streams of idolatrous blood by thy blood!

Rejoice, thou who wast thrown into boiling lead for Christ!

Rejoice, thou who wast sunk in the sea for His name!

Rejoice, thou who didst remain unharmed therein by the providence of God!

Rejoice, thou who didst pass through tortures of fire and water into the peace of Heaven!

Rejoice, thou who didst pour unfailing streams of mercy on the faithful!

Rejoice, gracious and compassionate physician who grantest healing through Grace!

Rejoice, Great Martyr and Healer Panteleimon!

KONTAKION 13

O, our long-suffering and wonderful Passion-bearer of Christ and Healer Panteleimon! Graciously accept from us this small offering, heal us of our many and various ailments, and through thy intercession protect us from enemies visible and invisible and pray to the Lord that we may be delivered from eternal torment, that we may continually sing in His Kingdom: Alleluia!

O, our long-suffering and wonderful Passion-bearer of Christ and Healer Panteleimon! Graciously accept from us this small offering, heal us of our many and various ailments, and through thy intercession protect us from enemies visible and invisible and pray to the Lord that we may be delivered from eternal torment, that we may continually sing in His Kingdom: Alleluia!

O, our long-suffering and wonderful Passion-bearer of Christ and Healer Panteleimon! Graciously accept from us this small offering, heal us of our many and various ailments, and through thy intercession protect us from enemies visible and invisible and pray to the Lord that we may be delivered from eternal torment, that we may continually sing in His Kingdom: Alleluia!

Most Holy Saint and Martyr Panteleimon-the-Healer, intercede to the Most Merciful God for *(NAME)* for the healing of his/her soul and body.

OIKOS 1

We know thee, glorious Panteleimon, as an earthly angel and a heavenly man. For adorned with angelic purity and martyrdom thou hast passed from earth to Heaven, where with angels and all the saints standing before the throne of the Lord of Glory, thou prayest for all of us on earth who venerate thee with these invocations:

Rejoice, torch of piety!

Rejoice, most glorious lamp of the Church!

Rejoice, adornment of venerable martyrs!

Rejoice, support of the faithful in unflinching endurance!

Rejoice, outstanding boast of youth!

Rejoice, warrior of Christ of invincible courage!

Rejoice, thou who having grown up in the world wast not of the world!

Rejoice, angel in the flesh, surpassing mortals!

Rejoice, all-blessed dweller in Heaven!

Rejoice, vessel of divine knowledge!

Rejoice, thou by whom faith has been exalted!

Rejoice, thou by whom delusion has been dethroned!

Rejoice, Great Martyr and Healer Panteleimon!

KONTAKION 1

Chosen passion-bearer of Christ and gracious healer, who freely grantest healing to the sick, we praise thee in songs as our protector. As thou hast boldness with the Lord, free us from all harm and sickness who cry with love to thee:

Rejoice, Great Martyr and Healer Panteleimon!

SELECTED PSALMS

PSALM 23 (22)

The Lord is my shepherd, I shall not want; He makes me lie down in green pastures.

He leads me beside still waters; He restores my soul.

He leads me in the paths of righteousness for His name's sake.

Even though I walk through the valley of the shadow of death, I fear no evil; for Thou art with me; Thy rod and Thy staff, they comfort me.

Thou preparest a table before me in the presence of my enemies; Thou anointest my head with oil, my cup overflows.

Surely goodness and mercy shall follow me all the days of my life; and I shall dwell in the house of the Lord forever.

PSALM 34 (33)

I will bless the Lord at all times; His praise shall continually be in my mouth.

My soul makes its boast in the Lord; let the afflicted hear and be glad.

O magnify the Lord with me, and let us exalt His name together!

I sought the Lord and He answered me, and delivered me from all my fears.

Look to Him and be radiant; so your faces shall never be ashamed.

The poor man cried, and the Lord heard him, and saved him out of all his troubles.

The angel of the Lord encamps around those who fear Him, and delivers them.

O taste and see that the Lord is good! Happy is the man who takes refuge in Him!

O fear the Lord, you His saints, for those who fear Him have no want!

The young lions suffer want and hunger; but those who seek the Lord lack no good thing.

Come, O sons, listen to me, I will teach you the fear of the Lord.

What man is there who desires life, and covets many days, that he may enjoy good?

Keep your tongue from evil, and your lips from speaking deceit.

Depart from evil, and do good; seek peace, and pursue it.

The eyes of the Lord are toward the righteous, and His ears toward their cry.

The face of the Lord is against evil- doers, to cut off the remembrance of them from the earth.

When the righteous cry for help, the Lord hears, and delivers them out of all their troubles.

The Lord is near to the Broken hearted, and saves the crushed in spirit.

Many are the afflictions of the righteous; but the Lord delivers him out of them all.

He keeps all his bones; not one of them is broken.

Evil shall slay the wicked; and those who hate me; I am spent by the blows of Thy hand.

When Thou dost chasten a man with rebukes for sin, Thou dost consume like a moth what is dear to him; surely every man is a mere breath!

Hear my prayer, O Lord, and give ear to my cry; hold not Thy peace at my tears!

For I am Thy passing guest, a sojourner, like all my fathers.

Look away from me, that I may know gladness, before I depart and be no more!"

PSALM 42 (41)

As a deer longs for flowing streams, so longs my soul for Thee, O God.

My soul thirsts for God, for the living God.

When shall I come and behold the face of God?

My tears have been my food day and night, while men say to me continually, "Where is your God?"

These things I remember, as I pour out my soul: how I went with the throng, and led them in procession to the House of God, with glad shouts and songs of thanksgiving, a multitude keeping festival.

Why are you cast down, O my soul, and why are you disquieted within me?

Hope in God; for I shall again praise Him, my help and my God!

My soul is cast down within me, therefore I remember Thee from the land of Jordan and of Hermon, from Mount Mizar.

Deep calls to deep at the thunder of Thy cataracts; all Thy waves and billows have gone over me.

By day the Lord commands His steadfast love; and at night His song is with me, a prayer to the God of my life.

I say to God my rock: "Why hast Thou forgotten me?

Why go I mourning because of the oppression of the enemy?" As with a deadly wound in my body, my adversaries taunt me, while they say to me continually, "Where is your God?"

Why are you cast down, O my soul, and why are you disquiet within me?

Hope in God; for I shall again praise Him, my help and my God!

PSALM 67 (66)

May God be gracious to us and bless us and make His face to shine upon us!

That Thy way may be known upon earth, Thy saving power among all nations.

Let the peoples praise Thee, O God, let all the peoples praise Thee!

Let the nations be glad and sing for joy, for Thou dost judge the people with equity and guide the nations upon earth.

Let the people praise Thee, O God; let all the peoples praise Thee!

The earth has yielded its increase; God, our God, has blessed us. God has blessed us; let all the ends of the earth fear Him!

PSALM 84 (83)

How lovely is Thy dwelling place, O Lord of Hosts!

My soul longs, yea, faints for the courts of the Lord!

My heart and flesh sing for joy to the living God!
Even the sparrow finds a home, and the swallow a nest for
herself, where she may lay her young, at Thy altars, O Lord of
Hosts, my King and my God!

Blessed are those who dwell in Thy house, ever singing Thy
praise!

Blessed are the men whose strength is in Thee, in whose
heart are the highways to Zion.

As they go through the valleys of Baca they make it a place of
springs; the early rain also covers it with pools.

They go from strength to strength; the God of gods will be
seen in Zion.

O Lord God of Hosts, hear my prayer; give ear, O God of
Jacob!

Behold our shield, O God; look upon the face of Thine
anointed!

For a day in Thy courts is better than a thousand elsewhere.

I would rather be a doorkeeper in the house of my God than
dwell in the tents of wickedness.

For the Lord God is a sun and shield; He bestows favor and
honor.

No good thing does the Lord withhold from those who walk
uprightly.

O Lord of Hosts, blessed is the man who trusts in Thee!

PSALM 134 (133)

Come, bless the Lord, all you servants of the Lord, who stand by night in the house of the Lord!

Lift up your hands to the holy place, and bless the Lord.

May the Lord bless you from Zion, He who made heaven and earth!

PSALM 138 (137)

I give Thee thanks, O Lord, with my whole heart; before the gods I sing Thy praise!

I bow down toward Thy holy temple and give thanks to Thy name for Thy steadfast love and Thy faithfulness!

For Thou hast exalted above everything Thy name and Thy word.

On the day I called, Thou didst answer me, my strength of soul Thou didst increase.

All the kings of the earth shall praise Thee, O Lord, for they have heard the words of Thy mouth; and they shall sing of the ways of the Lord, for great is the glory of the Lord.

For though the Lord is high, He regards the lowly; but the haughty He knows from afar.

Though I walk in the midst of trouble, Thou dost preserve my life; Thou dost stretch out Thy hand against the wrath of my enemies, and Thy right hand delivers me.

The Lord will fulfill His purpose for me; Thy steadfast love, O Lord, endures forever.

Do not forsake the work of Thy hands.

PSALM 148 (147)

Praise the Lord! Praise the Lord from the heavens, praise Him in the heights!

Praise Him, all His angels!

Praise Him, all His host!
Praise Him, sun and moon!

Praise Him, all you shining stars!

Praise Him, you highest heavens, and you waters above the heavens!

Let them praise the name of the Lord!

For He commanded and they were created.

And He established them for ever and ever; He fixed their bounds which cannot be passed.

Praise the Lord from the earth, you sea monsters and all deeps, fire and hail, snow and frost, stormy wind fulfilling His command!

Mountains and all hills, fruit trees and all cedars!

Beasts and all cattle, creeping things and flying birds!

Kings of the earth and all peoples, princes and all rulers of the earth!

Young men and maidens together, old men and children!

Let them praise the name of the Lord, for His name alone is exalted; His glory is above earth and heaven.

He has raised up a horn for His people, praise for all His saints, for the people of Israel who are near Him, Praise The Lord!

CONTEMPLATION BEFORE CONFESSION

Bless me, O Lord and my Savior, to confess to Thee not only with words but with bitter tears as well. There is much to weep for.

My faith in Thee is shaken, O Lord! The thoughts of little faith and faithlessness crowd into my soul more often than not. Why? Of course, the spirit of the times is guilty, the people with whom I associate are at fault, but above all, I myself am guilty, in that I do not struggle with faithlessness and do not pray to Thee for help; I am incomparably more guilty if I become a scandal for others by deed, by word, or by a cold silence, whenever conversations concerned the faith. I am sinful in this, Lord, forgive and have mercy and grant me faith.

Love for my neighbor and even for my close relatives fails me. Their incessant requests for help, their forgetfulness of how much has been done for them already, arouse mutual discontent among us. But I am guilty above all in that I have the means to help them, but help them grudgingly. I am guilty in that I help them, not out of pure Christian motives, but out of self-love, out of a desire for thanks or praise. Forgive me, Lord, soften my heart and teach me to look not at how people act towards me but at how I act towards them. And if they act in a hostile way, remind me, O Lord, to pay them back with love and good, and to pray for them!

I am also sinful in that I seldom, very seldom, think about my sins. Not only during week days, but even when preparing for Confession I do not remember them, do not strive to bring them to mind for confession. General phrases come to mind: "I'm not guilty of anything in particular, like everyone else." O Lord, it were as if I didn't know what sin is before Thee - that every vain word and the very desire in the heart is an abomination before Thee. And how many words and desires come each day, not to mention in a year! Thou alone, Lord, knowest them; do Thou grant me to behold my sins and be compassionate and forgive!

Moreover, I realize that my constant sin is the virtual absence of any struggle with evil within me. As soon as any excuse or suggestion appears, I already dive headfirst into the abyss of sin, and only after my fall do I ask myself: what have I done? A fruitless question, because it does not help me grow better. And if I feel sorrow at the same time, it comes from the fact that my self-love is wounded, and not from the awareness that I have offended Thee, O Lord! I do not struggle with obvious evil, nor even with the most trifling and harmful habits. I do not control myself and do not even try. I have sinned; forgive me!

Furthermore, there is the sin of having a short temper. This passion rules over me, does not leave me at all. When I hear a sharp word, I do not reply with silence, but act like a pagan: an eye for an eye and a tooth for a tooth. An enmity arises from something insignificant and continues for days and weeks, and I do not think of reconciliation, but rather try to be, as it were, stronger, to get revenge at the first chance. I have sinned beyond reckoning, O Lord, be compassionate, forgive me and put my heart at peace!

Apart from these major sins, my entire life is a chain of sins. I do not value the time which Thou hast granted for the acquisition of eternal salvation. I often stand irreverently, pray mechanically, judge others as to how they pray, and do not look after myself. At home I pray sometimes only with great effort and scattered thoughts, so that often I myself do not even hear my prayer, and I even omit my prayers sometimes. Such are my relations to Thee, O Lord, and I cannot say anything except: forgive and have mercy!

In my relations with others I sin with all my feelings - I sin with my tongue, by pronouncing false, profane, provocative and scandalous words; I sin with my eyes; I sin with my mind and heart. I judge o there and harbor enmity often and for long periods of time. I sin not only against the soul but also against the body, taking food and drink without restraint. Accept, O Lover of mankind, my repentance, that I may approach Thy holy and life-giving Mysteries with peace for the forgiveness of sins, for the setting-aright of temporary life and the inheritance of life eternal. Amen

"I am unworthy to ask forgiveness, O Lord," Thus exclaimed once the great teacher of repentance, Saint Ephraim the Syrian.

"How can one keep from falling into sin? How can one block the entrance to the passions?" Saint Basil the Great asked Saint Ephraim; and the answer was his tears alone. Then what can I say before Thee, O Lord, I so great and habitual a sinner? By the prayers of our holy Fathers Ephraim and Basil grant me, O Lord, repentance and tears! Help me to expel from myself, like deadly poison, my evil deeds, vain words, wicked thoughts. And if I forget to mention any sin, Thou knowest all, remind me, for I do not wish to hide anything. Thou commandest me: State your cause, that you may be justified *(Is. 43:26)*, and I say: my sins are multiplied Lord, and multiply themselves without ceasing, and there is no limit to them. I know and I remember, that even an impure thought is an abomination before Thee; and at the same time I not only think but even do that which grieves Thee. I know that I commit evil, and do not turn away from evil...

Thus, the beginning has not yet been made for my repentance, and the end is not in sight of my lack of concern over my sins. In truth, there is no end to the vile thoughts within me, the bursts of self-love, vanity, pride, judgments, bearing grudges and vengeance. I often argue, for no cause at all become angry, cruel, jealous, lazy, blindly stubborn. I myself am of very little significance, but I think a great deal of myself. I do not want to honor those who are worthy, but demand honor for myself without any basis. I constantly lie and am angry at liars. I condemn slanderers and thieves, but myself steal and slander. I corrupt myself with lustful thoughts and desires, but strictly judge others for lack of modesty. I do not endure jokes about myself, but myself like to tease others, considering neither the person nor the place - even in church. Whoever speaks the truth about me, I consider my enemy. I do not want to bother myself with serving others, but if I am not served, I grow angry. I coldly refuse my neighbor who is in need, but when I myself am in need, I make my requests of him without end. I do not like to visit the sick, but when I am sick, I expect someone to care for me without my even asking.

O Lord, send the light of Thy heavenly light into the depths of my soul, that I may see my sins! My confession almost always ends with the merely external recounting of certain sins. O my God, If Thou be not merciful, if Thou grant me not help, I perish! Innumerable are the times my conscience has given promises to Thee to begin a better life, but I violated my promises and live as before. Without correcting myself, I am ashamed to show my face before another person, before whom I have not kept my word. How then can I stand before Thee, my God, without shame and self-abasement, when I have made promises so many times before Thy holy altar, before the angels and saints, and then did not keep my word? How low I am! How guilty I am! Thine, O Lord, is righteousness, and mine is a shameful presence *(Dan.9:7)*. Only Thine infinite goodness can endure me. Thou didst not condemn me when I sinned; do not condemn me as I repent!

Teach me how to call to mind and recount the sins of my former life, the careless sins of youth the sins of self-loving adulthood, the sins of day and night, sins against Thyself, O Lord my Savior! How can I recount them in the few minutes when I stand in this holy place! I remember, Lord, that Thou didst attend to the brief words of the publican and the thief; I know that Thou wilt mercifully accept even the readiness to repent, and I pray Thee with all my soul, my Lord, accept my repentance, even in a daily confession of sins, according to the Prayer Book. I have far more sins than are mentioned in it, and have nothing with which to erase them.

I now offer only my striving towards Thee and the desire for good, but I myself do not have the strength to correct them myself. O Lord and Lover of mankind, Thou dost not drive away the sinner who comes to Thee, begging Thee for forgiveness. Even before he approaches the doors of Thy Mercy, Thou dost already open the way for him; even before he falls before Thee, Thou dost stretch forth Thy hand to him; even before he confesses his sins, Thou dost grant him forgiveness. Grant this to me, as I repent, grant this according to Thy great mercy; forgive all the evil that I have done, said and thought. And by granting forgiveness, send me, O Lord, the strength that henceforth I might live according to Thy will and not offend Thee. Help me, and I will be saved; help me by receiving Thy Holy Mysteries. And for the worthy reception of them, speak to me the grace of mercy and forgiveness through the lips of the servant of Thine altar, speak by Thy Holy Spirit not heard by the ear but heard in the contrite heart and peaceful conscience. Amen.

SOURCES

BY THE GRACE OF GOD, COMPILED AND ADAPTED FROM THE FOLLOWING SOURCES:

Orthodox Daily Prayers, Published by Saint Tikon's Seminary Press in 1982. No copyright registration; this book is in the Public Domain under Rule 5 of the U.S. Copyright Statutes.

Title: Orthodox Daily Prayers, Author: Anonymous, Release Date: January 16, 2011, PROJECT GUTENBERG No copyright registration; this book is in the Public Domain under Rule 5 of the U.S. Copyright Statutes.

Orthodox Prayer Book. Published by The Religious Education Department, Orthodox Church in America, Syosset, New York; 1979. No copyright registration; this book is in the Public Domain under Rule 5 of the U.S. Copyright Statutes.

Service of the Holy Orthodox Church, Classic version of Eastern Christian services and prayers, translated into English. Contains numerous liturgies, services and prayers from the Orthodox Church, published with the blessing of the Russian Church. Also includes explanations of services and the symbolism of church furnishings.

Non-Copyrighted Public Domain Prayers available freely online (multiple sites)

Many of the ruberics contained herein are paraphrased from the ruberics contained in multiple prayer books including the Old Orthodox Prayer Book, the Jordanville Prayer Book and the Holy Transfiguration Monastery Prayer Book. The text and format has been altered to prevent issues with "intellectual property". As a compilation which has been altered in keeping with U.S. Copyright law, portions of this work fall under "derivative works" and are fully legal for distribution by this author.